Praise for *Following Shimun*

T0279396

"In a language that derives its poetry from the landscapes that its author crosses, this story provides us with a double lesson in generosity, highlighting the sense of hospitality of the Innu, but at the same time reflecting Laure Morali's infinite gratitude to those who revealed it to her."

Dominic Tardif, *Le Devoir*

"[Laure Morali] gives us the moving chronicle of an encounter with a territory, a people, and an exceptional being in her story *Following Shimun*."

Marie-France Bornais, *Journal de Montréal*

"A very beautiful story. […] A magnificent, deeply human book."

Marie-Andrée Lamontagne, *Parking nomade* (Radio VM)

"During a journey through Innu territory, a woman meets an Elder who invites her to camp with him on the banks of the Manitou River, in the company of other Elders from the 11 Innu communities of the Quebec-Labrador peninsula. In the tent, fishing, or walking leisurely, the woman slowly learns her nomadic pace of life. Fall will soon take us back to hectic schedules, this story provides a great excuse to relax and is a magnificent tribute to Indigenous people."

Julie Roy, *L'actualité*

"A vibrant story."

Following Shimun

Laure Morali

translated by
HOWARD SCOTT

MAWEN<small>Z</small>I
HOUSE

Published with the generous assistance of the Canada Council for the Arts and
the Ontario Arts Council. We also acknowledge the support of the Government of
Canada through the Canada Book Fund and the Government of Ontario through
the Ontario Book Publishing Tax Credit.

We acknowledge the financial support of the Government of Canada through
the National Translation Program for Book Publishing, an initiative of
the Roadmap for Canada's Official Languages 2013-2018: Education,
Immigration, Communities, for our translation activities.

ONTARIO ARTS COUNCIL
CONSEIL DES ARTS DE L'ONTARIO
an Ontario government agency
un organisme du gouvernement de l'Ontario

Canada Council   Conseil des arts
for the Arts   du Canada

Canadä

Cover design by Sabrina Pignataro
Cover photo and photo on page ix by Laure Morali
Author photo by Sarah Rouleau

Library and Archives Canada Cataloguing in Publication

Title: Following Shimun / Laure Morali ; translated by Howard Scott.
Other titles: En suivant Shimun. English
Names: Morali, Laure, 1972- author | Scott, Howard, 1952- translator
Description: Translation of: En suivant Shimun.

Identifiers: Canadiana (print) 20240431103 | Canadiana (ebook) 20240431146 |
ISBN 9781774151716 (softcover) | ISBN 9781774151723 (EPUB) |
ISBN 9781774151730 (PDF)

Subjects: LCSH: Morali, Laure, 1972-—Travel—Québec (Province) | CSH:
Innu—Québec (Province)—Social life and customs | LCGFT: Travel writing.
Classification: LCC E99.I55 M6713 2024 | DDC 971.4004/9732—dc23

Printed and bound in Canada by Coach House Printing

Mawenzi House Publishers Ltd.
39 Woburn Avenue (B)
Toronto, Ontario M5M 1K5
Canada

www.mawenzihouse.com

For those who have walked in Nutshimit,

Nutshimiunnuat umenu

nitatamishkuauat mashinaikannu,

anitshenat ka pimuteht nete Nutshimit.

For the descendants of Shimun, who continue his path,

Nuenau, Lauraine, Christelle, Tania, Moïse-Pien,

Napessis, Tshiuetin, Maniu, Annick, Maniten, Nick-Pashin,

Julia-Uapikun, Ronny-Shikuan, and Shipek-Sébastien.

Contents

KUKAMESSIT

NUTSHIMIT

EKUANITSHIT

GULF OF ST LAWRENCE

TADOUSSAC

QUEBEC CITY

Preface

Laure Morali comes from the sea. For her, hope has an invisible colour and poetry is words without language. It is the sea wind that has brought her to us. She has slept on the moss and the lichen of Nutshimit. Shimun and his daughters, Nuenau and Penassin, passed on to her their love of the land.

Our home is Nutshimit. Spending three months inland with an Elder is the most beautiful journey you can take. It is a great honour when an Elder invites a person to go with him where he has lived his nomad life, and a demonstration of trust. He feels good in the company of that person who respects him. He wants to open up to that person the door to his true home, to the north, where all his riches lie, where he is one with nature. Where he is himself.

In our home, Nutshimit, we receive teachings by observing Elders, who transmit to us their knowledge in silence. We try to decipher their gestures. Elders communicate messages to us, and we become the bearers of those messages, so that the tradition is not broken. Silence is a teaching.

Laure Morali was invited to go into the woods by Shimun Pashin, a great hunter from the Ekuanitshit community with an unforgettable laugh and profound words. "When we lack respect for an animal, it is swallowed into the centre of the earth. The animals are disappearing, but one day, they'll come back," Shimun used to say.

In the eyes and the heart of Laure, Shimun recognized patience and open-mindedness, which one day would become a written page of his story. They canoed together among the islands of Lake Kukamess. They walked among the roots that feed the caribou, the leaves that travel to us and bring us the message that we must always remain faithful to the memory of the Ancients. In following Shimun, Laure Morali left the traces of her learning with the forest, the lake, the ice, the mountain, the animals, the fire, the wind . . . Nothing is forgotten when it is passed on.

Through the breath of words, an ancient path pulses, from heart to heart.

Rita Mestokosho, poet
Jean-Charles Piétacho, Innu chief
in Ekuanitshit

The Sky

Everything under the sky has an origin, and that origin could be called the mother.

Laozi

Memory of the Sky

I shouldn't be here today. Or maybe, quite the contrary, should I be precisely here, on this January 2, on the shoulder of the 175, waiting for a car to stop and take me north, hoping for a miracle, strength, love, the love that no one can give us or take away, because it doesn't come from anyone. With my three layers of sweaters and my parka, my shoulders must look very broad. If I stuff my hair under my tuque, I'll really look like a man and people will be reluctant to stop. Too bad! I'm cold.

I have blind faith in the names of places that pop into my head when I wake up, as if they'd fallen from a map of the sky and landed right in my dream. The beautiful mornings when that happens are too rare for me to forget them. Today is one of those beautiful mornings. A little tune is playing in my ear. Go to Mashteuiatsh, where the wind turns, where life is plain and simple. You will hear time taking its time and the source close to the source. There is wood, there is wind. There is air, there is fire. Go to Mashteuiatsh, where everything ends and everything starts again, find the magnet of your life.

A car finally stops. My mittens have had time to get stiff.

The right side of the man's face is marked by a long crease. It goes from below his eye down to his chin. He remains silent the whole time we are driving through the Laurentides Wildlife Reserve. When we get close to Chicoutimi, he pours out his whole story. "My wife asked me for a divorce six months ago. We were married for seventeen years. At the end of our life together, she let herself go. She didn't talk to me anymore. She didn't take care of herself. I don't know why she wanted to leave me . . . " His eyes are so clear that they reveal his bitterness and his blindness. Sadness has made him transparent. I allow myself to say to him, "That long wrinkle you have there looks like the path of a tear that was never shed."

As soon as we take to the road, encounters become mirrors. Barely a few hours after our New Year's embraces, he asked me to sit down with him, and said to me calmly, lowering his eyes, "I don't want a woman in my life." I packed my bag in the morning. Goodbye moiré gift wrap flying away in a gust of wind with the ribbon of the Pan-American highway, the dust of red deserts, the rumpled sheets of motels, the flowers thrown over the rims of canyons, where we would be fake married, but forever, goodbye screeches of the macaws in Mexican forests, deep voice of the adventurer interpreting the language of the birds, wooden love nest on a beach washed by the waves of the Pacific, salty smell of the skin, lustful looks shining like knife blades in the tension of eternal love at first sight.

The more we drive north, the more my vertigo intensifies. I feel the heart of a little star beating under my forehead. Mashteuiatsh, that name has a taste of premonition. It contains so many empty spaces that it looks like a loose section of the full score of the Word, memory of the land adrift in the sky. I feel like putting down my bag there, and letting myself be taken care of by the guardian spirit of polar places so it can heal my lost love blues under the blade of very pale days, a need to go through the big washing machine in the North to rid myself of old clothes of illusions. When I regain my strength, I'll continue my path in the direction of another cardinal point and take a long bath of wind rose.

Chicoutimi

I'm the only woman staying in the inn. The others, men of few words, are spending the winter renovating the property. I go out to get a bite to eat down by the river.

The Saguenay flows quietly a quartz black below the mountain. Promise of strength.

When I leave the inn, a young man with dark hair, very long, offers me his knife in a leather sheath as protection.

Mashteuiatsh

I arrive at the entrance to the village, and head on foot to the youth hostel by way of Uiatshuan Street. Silhouettes stroll by, snow in their souls, between the railway tracks. Deep down, I've always known that I would travel without a companion by my side this winter. I have the feeling I've set out in search of something I seem to have lost, I don't know what or when, but most likely a long time ago. The wind raises sails of purple snow in the mother-of-pearl shell, closed in by the sky, the frozen lake. The mirages unravel the mirages. In Mashteuiatsh, the dreams begin when they are brought to the forefront.

Aspens and alders surround the big dark wood building of the Auberge Kukum. Even if I wasn't going to be told it in the following hours, I would have thought it was haunted. The cat Orphée goes from one fireplace to another in the huge main room. The owner tells me that her mother-in-law Alphéda, the wife of the former band chief, has never left this home of hers, even after her death. She drifts from room to room, shrouded in a jade glow to light the way for spurned girls and lost travellers. The innkeeper suggests a trade: for room and board, I cook, I wash dishes, I welcome the rare customers, and I dust. That's exactly what I need. I'll have nothing to remind me of the time that is passing, noiselessly, in the recesses of existence.

The son of the house takes me for a walk with other children his age along the railway tracks, a boisterous band in yellow, orange, red, and green coats. Adam discovers a trail. "Uapush!" a hare went this way! We follow the fresh, bounding tracks of the uapush until we give up at a thicket. We let ourselves fall over backward and roll, roll down a snowy slope. Completely giddy, when we stand up, as the day is ending. Dogs are barking in the backyards. One of them, black with tawny eyes, joins the little troupe. Little girls are playing on a sheet of ice. Kéni hears the train. The song of the whistle floats in the air. Adam, Kéni, Napeu, Shan, the black dog, the little girls, and I in the mist of the blowing snow, have gazes like a starburst of rails. We could grab hold of a ladder, climb high up on a rail car, and set out like that, gliding on the setting sun.

Life in the inn is strange. One evening, while we're having tea by the fireplace with the owner and her friend Marco, the door opens on its own. Marco tries to reassure us: "Don't worry, it's just my father looking out for me."

Our destinations are written in secret. Dreams enrich the instincts that guide us. Some dreams take on the inner light of a rock painting. They are imprinted in the flesh to instill the body with its movement, and give breathing its rhythm. Eyelids start blinking like the wings of a butterfly magnetized by a light source. Those dreams, I believe them, through the wind, I believe them. There is always a dream to make a single one luminous among all the threads of the web of winds when it unfurls in the dawn. The heart opens up. A star on the forehead lights up. The route is given. Nothing more is heard but the crackling of the sky making its honey, like a swarm of bees. How not to believe, then, that very close to us there is an angel, the spirit of an animal, an ancestor?

> You dream, you go, you are.
> He dreams, he goes, he is.
> She dreams, she goes, she is.

I've been here for a month. Tomorrow, I'll go down to the St Lawrence and follow it to the end of the road.

The Wind Rose Is Making Waves

Route 138
February 1996

Great encounters happen by chance, if what we call chance also magnetizes the foreheads of birds whose hearts beat wildly when they come close to their pole. Destiny is a route that sings. With a talisman in my pocket, I listen to the messages of the wind through the openings in the bay windows in restaurants looking out on the icy St Lawrence.

The more I go forward, the more it grows, the big puzzle with blue cracks that forms the ice between the shores, stirring always. The currents push it to make and unmake itself, with the same power as a blade.

The ice advances on the river at the speed of clouds; it smells of the sea.

Tadoussac

I get to know Dean, a Māori traveller from New Zealand. He sees the invisible, the warriors who guide us.

The souvenir from Dean: that piece of varnished wood on which he has carved little leaves and written in three languages *The leaves of Putiputi*, "the leaves of Beauty."

Baie-Comeau

Rustling of dragonfly snow on the pink house: *Room to Rent.* A slim man wearing a cap is fixing his car in the yard. Does he rent rooms by the night?

"Usually it's by the month. Are you travelling alone?"

"Yes."

"You're pretty gutsy going for a stroll in the storm . . . And now you're here in Baie-Comeau where there's nothing to do, nothing to see. Okay, I'll give you the room for ten bucks a night."

I wash my clothes in the basement of the rooming house. The smell of winter, war painting, clings to my skin. The storms have tinted my memory by saturating it. They have left me bits of dawn, windows lit up like jewels, harvests of snow, hot water tinged with coffee in service stations, the spectrum of gazes in the mist on the windows when we leave each other, all those rivers . . . In the Chinese restaurant, Canadian cuisine, solitude is a blue that doesn't go away. Snow is cascading down. My finger on the starry path of drops of coffee, I watch this future flowing by like a cartoon strip on oilcloth. The route of the winds is the one the nomads take when they go find their future.

The storm still shrouds Baie-Comeau. Can people see me from their cars? My hands and feet are cold. The Subway sign provides a touch of yellow in all that white. In the distance, the letters of Dunkin' Donuts fade to pink on the flakes lit by the headlights of vehicles, but I don't feel like anything sweet. I decide to look for a little warmth in the Subway and order a BLT submarine. I feel uneasy when the waitress asks me to make quick choices: mayonnaise? vinegar? pickles? onions? olives? mustard? peppers? She looks annoyed by my hesitations when I don't have time to think, so I say yes to everything without realizing that I was completely spoiling my meal by mixing all those flavours. Senior citizens, each at their own table, are sipping watery coffee. I sit down at one of the orange Formica booths by the window. Everywhere on the coast, whether in a mining town like Baie-Comeau, a fishing port like Matane, a town surrounded by forests like Forestville, old men and women spend hours at the cold tables of shopping centres. They have faces marked by the work they had to do taming and clearing the wilderness, hollow cheeks, protruding chins, very wrinkled foreheads. Their gazes seem translucent. Their insides are steeped in the humility that nature has taught them. Their children have migrated to Montreal or Quebec City, as if, in this land of storms, the parents did not have enough feathers to reassure their broods. A bitter taste mixes with the flavour of the coffee served in a cup that warps on contact with the hot liquid. A question, always the same, intrudes forcefully: what am I doing here? Here, on the Côte-Nord, the North Shore of the St Lawrence, when I grew up on northern shores, as if I had crossed to the other side of the looking glass. On my little peninsula nestled between two bays, I spent my time looking past the islands, strung out on the horizon, trying to see the other side of the sea. The tide would ebb, the emerald water running over the sand, I would follow the flow to the end of the foreshore. By following the current, I ended up putting to sea. I packed my bags with the necessary nonchalance, with the right balance of fear and desire. I entered my latitude, 48° 35′ N. I could see Saint-Malo and Saint-Jacut-de-la-Mer a little more to the west from my porthole. I had a lump in my throat. The ocean margin created the gap where I could put forgetting. Where I come from, winter barely exists. Where I am, it's really very cold. What am I doing here, in the Subway in Baie-Comeau, at minus thirty by the side of the road with the windchill brought by passing trucks? This thought makes me smile. And what should I do with this backpack, so big, wedged between two chairs? I finish the little packet of potato chips included with the "trio six-inch submarine, potato chips, soft drink." I crush my cigarette in the aluminum ashtray. I put on the coat, the tuque, the scarf, and the straps of the backpack. If I don't know what I'm doing here, I know at least that I don't want to stay. We give ourselves up to the road as we give ourselves up to the sea.

The driver of the black car I get into is an Innu policeman from Mani-utenam. Why not go where he's going . . . I ask him about the prospects for lodgings in his community. He doesn't answer. I recite to him the few words that I know in Innu-aimun, hoping he'll like that. He remains frosty and drops me at the entrance to Sept-Îles, in the parking lot of the Galeries Montagnaises shopping centre, at the corner of Laure Boulevard. Quite a landing! A sheet of black ice helps me to appreciate, my face on the ground, the mood of the road with which I share my first name.

The owner of the youth hostel was getting ready to go home. I'm his only client in months. He leaves me the keys to the place. The night falls quickly. I go out to buy a can of soup. Forgotten Christmas lights dangle from buildings, trying to drown winter under their aquatic green glow. In the port, ice imprisons the cargo ships. The islands line the horizon with seven strokes. The cold cuts through my skin. I go back to the hostel to heat up the soup.

It's so strange to sleep among dozens of bunkbeds, all empty. To populate this gloomy place, I imagine an angel sitting on the edge of each bed. When I'm half asleep, a dream pops up in a fraction of a second, like an image from a cartoon: a red car brakes abruptly in front of me on the highway. I get up with the strange feeling that I have to take my time getting out of the city. I have to make room in my backpack, because today I'm going to receive a present, but it's a surprise. The thought makes me feel very light.

The road rises under the pencil line edge of the woods. It fades away through a snowy sheet of light. I squeeze my fingers in my palms like a fruit fallen from the sky, instinct. The hours go by at the exit to Sept-Îles, until twelve-thirty and ten seconds, the instant when snowmobiles jostle my luggage. One of the drivers beckons me to get on behind him. I point to my bag, too big for his seat. He suggests I get into the red pickup which is following with the gear. I climb in beside the white-haired driver. Before speeding off, the snowmobilers tell us to meet them at the restaurant on the river Mishta-shipu.

I take the time, during the meal, to observe one by one the ten Acadians, bundled up in their suits. I try to read their hearts through their faces. Is it risky to make a stop with them, tonight, at the motel in Rivière-au-Tonnerre then continue the journey together to Havre-Saint-Pierre? With their good-natured smiles, they seem already to consider me like their little sister of the road and offer to take me to the end of the 138 by snowmobile.

At the Jonathan Motel, the mascot of which is the famous seagull, the proprietor unfolds a cot for me in the room of the two veterans of the group. From that night, I retain one lesson: the whiteness of a head of hair has nothing to do with the expression "as pure as the driven snow"; from my bed, I had to raise my voice to silence the insistent entreaties of the driver of the red pickup.

The road hangs by a thread, a trembling of heartstrings, the St Lawrence is wider and wider—here they say the sea—and the forest is thinning into the taiga. To the swaying of black spruce, the ice is channeled into the Gulf of St Lawrence, a container ship brushes past Anticosti Island, the areas of skin that I have not been careful to cover freeze under the burn of the full-force wind. The snowmobiles speed along an endless beach. Snowbathed children wave to me laughing under the shimmer of sky-blue sheets—speeding up the beating of my heart—what is this village? Mingan . . . Ekuanitshit . . .

The road ends at Havre-Saint-Pierre and the snowmobile trail to Natashquan has not been cleared since the last storm. The snowmobilers decide to turn back.

"And the little lady, what'll she do now?"

"Drop me in Ekuanitshit."

Night is falling. Only the police station has the lights on. I'll ask there.

The policeman bursts out laughing, looking up from his files.

"You don't remember me? I picked you up hitchhiking in Baie-Comeau the other day. I gave you a lift to Sept-Îles."

"You again!"

"What can I do for you today?"

"I'd like to find a room in Ekuanitshit."

"Impossible. No tourists, no strangers. No one sleeps like that on the reserve."

He smiles with the satisfaction of having fulfilled his role, denying me access to all the Innu communities in the land. Enough is enough! He's already made it clear he didn't want to see me in Mani-utenam, and now in Ekuanitshit. But I haven't fallen into the well of Alice in Wonderland so that the same character is multiplied and appears everywhere along my route. If someone is trying to test my determination, he won't be disappointed. I'll come back.

The snowmobilers, who suspected that the police station was not an information tourist office, have waited for me. In Longue-Pointe-de-Mingan, the next village, they know a bed-and-breakfast with nice rooms. It's here that the red pickup, the snowmobiles, and my backpack go their separate ways.

I sleep like a log for fifteen hours after coming up against the end of the road like a solid mirage.

At noon, I meet Manon, who is staying in the next room. She teaches in Ekuanitshit and offers to go with me to the school. Today is the carnival. I smile at the idea of seeing the face of the policeman if he notices me. The children are busy building a fort with blocks of hard snow in front of the school. I mix with a group. All morning I swim in a tide of laughter. The children of Ekuanitshit bring me a joy such as I've rarely known. That comes from far away, maybe from the future.

I escape towards the sea. The turquoise ice capsizes in the salt water with hissing sounds. An eagle circles over the tops of the fir trees on the island. The strength of its wings presses down on my shoulders. I fall to my knees in the snow.

There are roads you dip into just to change clothes in the end.

The Sea

That noon
Life was so unsettling and so good
that you told it or rather whispered
"go away and lose me wherever you want"
The waves answered "you won't come back from it"

NICOLAS BOUVIER

Shimun's Family

Ekuanitshit
Uapikun-pishim", the moon of flowers
June 1996

With Manon's help, I proposed to the Ekuanitshit Innu Council that I conduct poetry and theatre workshops for young people with Fabienne, my childhood friend turned actor. I was given the good news by telephone that the project had been accepted. We will be housed with someone in the community in exchange for our workshops. Fabienne came from Brittany and met me in Montreal and we set off with our bags and our spring laughter—three days to hitchhike a thousand kilometres.

With Moon and The King, two fishermen from Havre-Saint-Pierre, we ride along the gulf from Sept-Îles, our hair in the wind, the two of us among the lobster pots in the back of their pickup. They drop us at the general store. The children appear as if by magic. Their bicycles encircle us. A young boy yells: "I know where you're going to live, at Penassin's place, the house over there, beside the church!" I don't know if it's from fatigue or from the joy of finally being back, but I can't stop laughing. Escorted by the children on bikes, we go across the village under loads of freshly washed laundry hanging on pulley

clotheslines behind the houses. Canoes turned over on wooden
stakes touch the sky with their hulls. An old woman, on her
knees in the grass, is tending to a fire. She's going to bake her
bread under a thick layer of sand. The children stop at the red
canteen, then leave us to go say hello to the whales at the end
of the pier. The sun beats down, the laundry floats. Trucks go
by on the 138. On the porch of her white house, Penassin, pink
tank top and dark glasses, is listening to the radio. She was
waiting for us. Over a cup of coffee, she tells us what's what:
"I'm a woman of action. You'll often see people come by here.
I'm a social worker. I take care of the needs of people who want
to go into therapy. But I'm not all alone. We work as a team to
solve the problems of the community. That's my life." She has a
smile that says she knows a lot about the areas of shadow and
light inside people.

Penassin takes us to supper with her father Shimun and her
sister Nuenau who live in the tundra green house on the other
side of the 138. Nuenau is brewing the tea. She stirs the sugar
with a spoon in a little pot of amber-black liquid. Later she
takes a shower and wraps a water-green towel from the kitchen
cupboards around her wet hair. Shimun is wearing a green tank
top, almost emerald in the shadows of the waning day. He is
watching a documentary on animal life in the Amazon. He rolls
himself a cigarette with one sand-and-ember hand while rocking in his rocking chair. Mischievous eyes sparkle behind his
glasses. I feel like smiling for no reason. His presence gives me a
strong feeling of happiness as if I were finding a brother in the
skin of a grandfather. The last sparkles of the day scatter around

the clothesline in the yard. Everything seems suspended, the line, the heavy sun, the reason for being here, Nuenau's forearm, the tobacco that is no longer being consumed in the rolled cigarette, Shimun's gaze floating between nostalgia for the forest and the hope that he places in the younger of his daughters to occupy the territory—he raised her like a man who hunts. Even the hand of the watch on his left wrist seems to have stopped beating. But maybe he's not really watching the television. Maybe he's thinking of buying a bingo card for the game that will start at seven o'clock on the community radio, or else the caribou leg that he'll have to thaw out for the next day's dinner. Maybe he's wondering like me where the impression of having already experienced this moment comes from, balanced in the disquiet of affection. He holds himself like an actor taking a deep drag of tobacco before turning back to the observing eye.

"Before 'Indians,' what was it they called us? 'Savages' . . . Hidden in the woods all the time, 'savages'!" And he starts laughing, a yellow *uashtessiu* laugh of the moon while the land is lit up, carpeted with larch needles, the Innu going deep into the taiga, little children's heads hidden in the bottoms of their canoes—those ones won't be going to the residential schools. His contagious laugh dries into a hoarse stream. The coughing fit makes me laugh less. "I've got tons of tobacco!"

In one hand strong like a paddle grip, he rolls another cigarette between two fingers yellowed by brown tobacco. I would follow him anywhere.

"We'll go all over. The forest. The river. The sea. And the animals . . . "

Shimun has us taste his caribou stew, accompanied by a piece of bannock and a nice cup of tea. The forest melts in our mouths. Nuenau radiates a gentle assurance. She has auburn hair and laughs as she tells us that when she was little her parents convinced her she had been found in the lodge of beavers whose fur is like the colour of her hair. Shimun's wife, who passed away last year, left an emptiness that Nuenau is trying to fill with her attentions.

Maniten, Shimun's mother, lives a few blocks away in a straw-yellow wooden house that smells nice, with the wood burning in the stove, the caribou meat, and the caribou hide she is tanning to make her crafts. In a frame, this image of the sky: day is breaking, the old pink of roses falls in Mary's hands. From Maniten's lips comes a song, from the window to the stove, from tea to bread, from the ashtray to the TV, from the cabinet drawer to the kitchen table . . .

> Mani miam uapikun
> Like a rose, Marie

She takes bags out of a cookie tin, pours seed beads into a saucer, pierces a piece of smoked caribou leather. Maniten strings the beads onto the needle, the yellow ones for the heart, the blue for the morning and the water, and for the petals, the purple. With nomad memory, she embroiders paths and rivers on the moccasins. She gives her footsteps to the feet of the village children; they will still be raising snow in the wind of the animal.

Maniten is the strongest, smallest, and most gentle woman

I know. She soars into the sky every time she looks at you. Worried about not seeing right away the blue deep in your heart, her eyes blink. When she touches it above your face, she is no longer looking at anything but it. Her smile, then, no longer vanishes.

At night, Penassin stays up late drinking tea. She invites us to sit by the window and talks to us in a low voice about the power of the dreams that guide her. "There are two worlds, the world of dreams and the world we live in. The line between the two is thin. It comes to life through our spirits. The thread that links us to what surrounds us is stitched by our beliefs. There are things that we see with our eyes and others with our souls. The two are inseparable. The night gives me strength. Dreams make me grow. They show me what will happen. I travel far and I come back with knowledge about life, about death. On waking, everything is clear. I'm not in a hurry. I know which path to take. I'm rarely surprised by what happens. I knew you would come. When I open my door, it's for life."

Every day since our arrival, Fabienne has been leading the theatre workshops while I take the other part of the group fishing for poems. I don't feel much older than my young students and my poetry workshops are without discipline. Lying on the pier, fingers fluttering in the water to imitate fish, the children attract the whales with pink and black bellies. It's to the rhythm of the leaps of the little minke whales, where the water is the deepest, a few metres from the wharf, that poems appear like this one by Lauraine:

Eternal love
unforgettable hope
the flower has a planet
the moon full of joy

calm nature
the magic of love
the sacred feather
the universal path

the spirit of our people
the round earth

Shimun, his heart like a topographic map, rocks in his red checkered chair. He does not understand why the Whites went to "so much trouble" to convert the Innu, so then today young people like us turn up with no religion. "Don't you believe in anything anymore?" For him, I'm a lost cause. Not only do I not have children yet, but I'm neither baptized nor married. What kind of a scam is this? "I'm going to call Father Delaunay to have you baptized!" He's afraid for my soul.

Shimun lays shreds of tobacco in the rolling paper with his hardened fingers. "Tshakapesh lives in the moon, he lives in the moon, Tshakapesh, able to walk on the water and catch the eagles!" Shimun says to us raising his eyes to the sky. Tshakapesh is the one whose parents were devoured by a mammoth bear when he was still in the belly of his mother. His sister found his fetus in the snow. She placed him in a cauldron. Tshakapesh grew up in a few instants. Thanks to this power that he had to grow and shrink at will, Tshakapesh was able to elude the traps of the giant beavers, ogresses, and strangers against which his sister had warned him. One day, when he had again disobeyed her and had gone off to hunt squirrels far from the camp, his arrow got stuck among the branches of a tree. Tshakapesh climbed into the tree, blew on it, and the tree grew. Tshakapesh climbed higher still, blew, and the tree grew. The tree grew all the way to the moon, that magnificent country where Tshakapesh chose to rest. He went to get his sister, but she decided to stay on the sun. He preferred to live on the moon. He's still there. He can be seen, when the moon is full,. drawing his bow, Tshakapesh, the first man to have walked on the moon.

By telling us the story of Tshakapesh, Shimun gives us an idea for a play we'll create with the children. Their poems naturally find places among the dialogues of the play. The performance takes place in front of the families in the community hall. At the end of the show, the cardboard moon falls on the fir tree, which falls on the little canvas tent. The collapse of the scenery causes an explosion of laughter.

Our project has come to an end. Fabienne has to return to Brittany. I take the ferry to villages farther east, beyond the road. I promise the children, and Penassin, Nuenau, Shimun, and Maniten, that I will come back to see them soon.

On a bench on board the *Nordik Express*, in my sleeping bag that night, I watch the canvas of my life float by and stretch out.

Light Blues

The same beach borders the world
the blue, the space.

The boat moors at dawn. We are only three passengers disembarking. The others, pale and red-headed, English-speaking, are continuing the journey to Blanc-Sablon, the final destination of the *Nordik*. On the pier, the people are looking for packages, fish, disembarking travellers. I have scribbled the name Lisa, the cousin of an Ekuanitshit friend, on a piece of cardboard.

Lisa sets the bread on the table. Slices of salmon are sizzling in a frying pan. Jean-Claude pours hot tea into our glasses. The silence spreads puddles on the tablecloth. Little Doris with big hazel eyes and a necklace of blue plastic beads is playing with the salmon on her plate. "We eat it every day," Lisa explains. I glance out the window. An old man kneeling in the sand spreads a white canvas over the hull of his canoe. Tents are steaming behind the houses. The freshly repainted canoes are drying in the smoke of fires.

Jean-Claude's words suddenly start up like flying sparks: "One day in November, up there in the North, on a frozen lake, there were five of us on the trail of a bear. Its tracks went off in all directions on the lake. I thought about it. The lair could only be in one place: facing the sun throughout the day, from when it rises until it sets. I followed one of the trails by turning my back to the sun. I went straight to the lair. I killed the bear, a black bear, very big . . . You know, my father told me everything, he told me everything about the shaking tent. It was a very small tent pitched on wooden poles. The trees themselves talked to The One who has the power of the Spirit, to tell him to choose their branches of alder or white spruce. The man called the Kakushapatak entered the tent. The others stayed outside. We could hear the chant of the clouds come down. The tent started moving and spinning, very fast. Inside all the animals were calling: goose, bear, caribou, moose, otter, tortoise, eagle, marten, all the animals, even the black fly. All the Masters of the animals were with him. And Kakushapatak was seen inside."

I walk without knowing where I'm going, in the soft blues of the dust raised by the pickups in the sandy streets. Clean sheets are swinging in the salty air. On the wooden porches, people take the time to drink in the sun and the shadow. Portable radios transmit the bingo results. The words slide by without unravelling anything, flowing from the river where the salmon run. The sea hits the dunes.

I take the boat again. Lisa had informed Paule, her Unaman-shipu cousin, of my arrival. The light is heady. I'm tempted to sink into life like the buzzard in the forest searching for a sensation of shadow. Innocence close to desire overruns the landscape. The sea recedes. The waves are breaking over the deck. The ocean pushes the blue back to the night shore.

The Ochre River

Unaman-shipu
La Romaine
July 1996

The motorboat pounds against the waves, cuts through in-between the many islands, round and grey, covered with water-green lichen. Lisa's cousin Paule and her husband Shan-Kanut take me camping with their children. The vegetation is so short that Jacques Cartier compared this land to the one that God gave Cain—he certainly did not bend down in the taiga to gather the *shikuteua*, those delicious orange fleshy marsh berries that grow in the islands on the lobster rocks. The name of the lake on the shores of which we are going to camp derives from that fiery fruit. We make our way inland by Unaman-shipu, the Ochre River.

A little rain is falling on Lake Uashikute. Wood is burning in the stove. The heat cools when it goes past the rolled-up canvas door of the tent. Tani is sleeping on the foam mattress. Shan-Kanut cuts potatoes into thin slices that he grills directly on the stove griddle. We're resting after fishing. We pass around tea in a miniature pot. The sky mixes its storm smell with the fragrance of the fir-branch carpet. The trout are drying with our shoes, hanging on the stick above the stove. Shan-Kanut goes out in the night to check the nets. I have a dream in which an eel devours fish. Shan-Kanut comes back empty-handed—nets torn by razor-sharp teeth.

As July 26 approaches, we head back down to the mouth of the river. A big gathering Saint Anne's feast day is being prepared in Kami, "the other side" of the river. The boats come and go between Kami and the village, people bringing clean clothes, candles, pots, dishes. The gazes of Elders kneeling in the bottoms of the boats cut through the mists. Flags with invented designs are flying above the tents. Fish is smoking on wooden sticks. In the wind of summer and the thirst of summer, flour, salt, and water run between the fingers of the women. The bread crackles as it cooks under fire in the sand. The mist lifts the songs of the five o'clock Mass, the craggy cadences of Innu-aimun. A statue of Saint Anne under glass stands on the hull of the overturned canoe that will be used as an altar. In her arms, she is holding her daughter in a lapis-lazuli dress.

Paule takes me to the tent of her mother, Anne, who says hello to me. She looks a little over my shoulder, in the distance, and lets the wind come and set a few notes on her lips, to outline a smile. Her long silver hair gathered in a purple ribbon sparkles on a pale green cotton jersey. A pink and white apron covers her earth-coloured skirt. Her movements extend those of her companion Thomas, when she grabs the logs he has just split, when she puts them in the fire under the grille, when she threads the trout onto the stick he sets over the embers, the trout he cuts open and cleans.

Evening in the tent, where light sheets hang to protect us from mosquitos, Anne feeds the wood stove, takes out tobacco and the pipe, lights it as if she were alone and far away, in the heart of the ages. She goes outside. I follow her. I smoke a cigarette, and she, the pipe. As we listen to the children, we can hear their thirst for play waning. The canvas of the tents made transparent by the flames of the candles is willing, at ground level, to be the only beacon in the night.

We get up at dawn in the camp. The first fires have been lit. Echoes of dreams vanish in the ashes. The wind blows in the flags. The weather is grey on the barrens. The banners flap. Today is July 26. The gravelly voice of an Elder rises on the taiga. The men, caps on their heads, and the women, wearing berets of red and black beaded fabric congregate. Paths, rivers on which flowers and canoes float. On a table they place statuettes of Saint Anne, candles, rosaries, medallions, spring water, sea water for the healing to come. The priest comes out of his cabin. His alb floats on the wind. He sprinkles incense over the objects. Brittany comes back to my eyes, transparent wind rose in the mist enveloping the islands, the moors, the gazes, the smiles, and the tears. Saint Anne, the Grandmother, is loved on both sides of the ocean.

The end of one world is the beginning of another. The gateway to the East, reddened by rising suns, gives us at every moment the courage to fulfill our paths. The same blood of prayers bubbles in the Finistère. But over there, we are peninsula dwellers focused on the death of the sun, like old sages, sitting in the house of the West, who watch the path travelled inside themselves.

The Elders are believers just as the rock in the river believes in the spring that it feels running against its walls. The wind confides in them about shores where life is written, and the words circulate in the veins of the earth. After the Mass this noon, the Elders honour Papakassik[u], the Master of Animals, with a feast of caribou fat—he will draw for them fire maps on the shoulder blades heated in the embers, which will open the path of his herds.

Here, in the Innu summer garden that is fire, meat, canvas, fish, star, I love this wind that runs through my fingers.

Spirit River

Ekuanitshit
Upau-pishimu, the moon when the young ducks
take flight for the first time
August 1996

"So, does it feel good to come home again?" Penassin opens the door to me. She couldn't have made me happier.

Shimun invites me to go camp with him on the shores of the Manitou River. The Elders of eleven Innu communities from the Quebec-Labrador peninsula gather this week in Ekuanitshit. I find Anne, Thomas, and many others whom I've met in Unaman-shipu and Nutashkuan. We smile at each other in silence. The gathering of Elders is the story of lives, the murmur of the territory. Everything told by the faces is written elsewhere in the stones, the traces of a fire, of a camp, in the trees that remember having given branches for fire, needles for beds, the fragrance. All the forces are there, promised. The smoke of cooking fires carries aromas of duck, goose, caribou, beaver . . . There's no hurry. The wind stirs like a passing branch—this wind that is a legend, a source, words from Nutshimit.

William-Mathieu Mark bends over, his face to the drum, his hand on the stick, his heart in the belly of the drum. The drum: the skin of the caribou, the bones of the caribou that vibrate along the leather cord strung across the circle. A woman stands up from a bench, takes small steps towards the centre of the community tent, starts the dance. Her face held very high, hues of the wind in her eyes, snow in her movement, ground beneath her feet, she dances to the rhythm of her heart. Her arms beat against her thighs like the wings of a wild goose. It is eternity, dream, voice mixing, the tangible emotion of laughter. We remember: the endless walking, the ground, the paths. The circle erases and starts again the memory of lives. A woman, a man, a woman . . . I have often made love, the woman who is dancing the makushan seems to say. I have often walked, I have often loved, and I am full of all those memories. I am a full life. I understand the signals of the wind, sensitive, my body is sensitive.

The voice of William-Mathieu Mark comes from the belly and from a mountain striated with veins when his stick strokes the caribou skin and the bones resonate along the leather.

The tents are lit up like fireflies. "Why do you think the old people play the drum?" Shimun asks me as he relights the fire in the stove. "It's for the animals! The old people, when they went to bed in the evening, made the drum reverberate, the animals, they saw all that. You have to have the drum dream three times in order to be able to make the drum, to play the drum and see fire being lit in the circle at the place where the caribou herd is found. You have to dream three times."

The wind carries the dust of words that are the memory of the most distant past, like the most distant future; the dream, a painting that navigates in the night.

The rain drips through the morning smoke, the laughter under the tents, the noise of axes. A child is crying. In the shadow of a blue tarp, a woman is washing herself. Another is mixing sand with ashes in the fire before laying the bannock dough there. The smell of porcupine that has smoked all night long over the embers lingers close by. A radio crackles. This wind that is a heritage of the days, a resolution of promise, it is the goodwill of the North, East, South, and West brought together by an inner breeze, life, nothing but life.

A floatplane flies over the camp. Shimun follows it with his eyes. When autumn comes, it will be time to climb into the plane, which will carry the families farther north, drop them off on the shore of a lake, for the time of animals, of traps, of walking on paths. When September comes, the airplane will come . . .

The Colour Green

I have not known the sea
below Anticosti
in the shadow of Mingan Island
cabins balancing
on the rounded rocks

we would pull back light curtains in the three-o'clock sun
watch the sea lions stick their heads out of the waves
their backs smooth and wet like those stones
gathered from the river bed
for the evening ceremony

I drank the black bag tea that the Elders like
after trading it many times at the trading posts
of the Hudson Bay for the fur
of a silver fox

the cloudberries
crackling hot bread in the sand
under the fire I did not know
the sea in the hands of old women
who gather eider eggs
on islands at summer's end

coming out of the forest as if from a nest
the sea with them that was the journey
that had to be undertaken
across Nutshimit
they taught me the name of the sea
Shipek[u], the colour green Shipeku

on the barrens with its velvety leaves
in the evening Maniten with the sun red scarf
invited me to go with her frail at a hundred years
to call the whale cradling the spirit of the water

I did not recognize the sea in her eyes
I saw life expand
to the edges
of the world

the Gulf of St Lawrence
the taiga my hands full
of Labrador tea
drunk on the sound of big
marine mammals

the northern lights sponge
the fever of my flights
in the Milky
Way of childhood

around the Pole Star
like the She-Bears
returned

Mingan
a small island
and old friends

I was there
for no reason
like the sea.

The Land

A vision of you
voyage in a land
at the infinite limits
of your belief.

JOSÉPHINE BACON

The Moon When the Land Lights Up

Ekuanitshit
Uashtessiu-pishim[u]
October 1998

October 1

Shimun is waiting for the wind to die down so that the plane can take us inland. For the last week, the storm has kept us in the house among bags and boxes. We have to keep ready for the pilot's call. We've bought food supplies to last at least two months in the woods. I've been given a pair of snowshoes woven with strips of rawhide. Maniten knitted me wool socks and made me a hat of arctic hare fur. Nuenau loans me one of her pairs of knee-high moccasins that she stuffs into my bag saying: "You can't know how good we feel in Nutshimit. We walk, we paddle, we admire the lake, the mountains, we hunt, we cut our wood, we don't stop for an instant." Shimun's face lights up. This is no longer the same man. "You have to come with us to understand."

"The forest is the house of our father," adds Penassin, who helps me roll up the foam mattresses so they can be stuffed into big canvas bags.

Nutshimit, October 5

Axes, guns, tents, blankets, bags of clothes, saws, dogs pour into the Beaver floatplane. The lakes spread out, the rivers appear, the mountains are discovered. Shimun unfolds the map of his memory before our eyes. In less than two hours, we have flown the three hundred kilometres that took more than a month to travel in canoe by the rivers. He would leave the shore of the sea at the end of summer with his parents and his siblings and arrive at Lake Kukamess during the moon when the land lights up. They would spend the whole of autumn there before continuing on foot by the frozen lakes to Nanim, "the other North," as far as Ungava Bay. In the spring, they would return.

Kukamess-nipi

51° 51′ 32″ N, 64° 13′ 0″ W

The airplane alights by the shore of Lake Kukamess. It offloads our baggage at the water's edge and takes off again. Shimun and his son Shamani go off to cut little spruce trees which they strip to pitch the prospector tent. Penassin shows me how to gently remove from the fir trees their branches swollen with needles, with one quick hand movement. We sink them into the earth, all in the same direction, we braid a fragrant carpet that will protect us from the damp of the ground. Shimun puts together the pieces of the wood stove. He inserts the stovepipe through a hole cut for that purpose in the tent canvas. Nuenau teaches me how to carry long logs on my shoulder—one third in front and two thirds behind. We cut them up at the campsite. That makes nice music, the noise of the saw interspersed with our laughter . . . Shamani splits blocks of wood in four and we pile up the firewood inside the tent. Shimun lights the first fire. We cook the meal on the stove. I'm falling down with fatigue.

October 6

We wake up at five in the morning. A layer of snow covers the boreal moss. I gaze at the lake and the wind. Everything is vast and calm. We carry containers filled with water to the tent. Shamani puts up shelves above our mattresses for our toiletries, our books, and our talismans.

October 7

Misty weather. Snow covers everything. The lake is silver. The woods are shining. The paddle against stone drives the canoe. Shimun directs, I lead the way. Only our arms are working. The spruce trees sway gently along the shore.

So old, so new, the world of Shimun never stops pretending to end at the far side of the islands, heavy with life, carried to the sky by the fir trees. During the portage across an arm of land, Shimun sets an otter trap. On the other side, we paddle past a big island. We go by Pikuanipanan, the Place where one casts a net under the winter ice.

Shimun rolls himself a cigarette. "I've got tons of tobacco!" he exclaims, amused as he is every time he comes out with one of his leitmotifs. Who is he speaking to, through me?

We are going around a narrow curve. Three islands fill the horizon. The canoe works its way against a countercurrent. The northern portion of the lake comes into view:

Big Lake Kukamess, where the lake trout are abundant.

It makes me think of the sea, with its great wind that whips lines of snow and leaves us with red on our cheeks and islands hazy in the mist. Three ducks scratch the sky, escaping like arrowheads. We will be the last migratory species to stay behind waiting for winter.

The shadowy vessel of an island seems to drift in the distance beneath the fast-moving clouds packed full of snow. Waves swell the lake.

We go up a stream, pull the canoe onto the bank, go into the forest wet with heavy snow. Shimun knows where he's going. He picks up a piece of freshly cut shrub. His face relaxes and lights up: "All right, I found the beaver!"

October 8

It snows during the night.

The white refreshes my spirit this morning. I wash at the lake. Three months will go by quickly. I promise myself I'll take advantage of every instant. My body day after day will become tougher, my sight will soar farther. The skins of hares crumble as they fall, separate into straw-white sparks and dissolve slowly, melt into the icy water where the snow appears hot; a white fire that will close in until it forms a reassuring blanket around our bodies. On the CB radio, the word *kun*, "snow," is retransmitted to the coast. There, people are dreaming of living under the tent, door open to the lake, watching the snowflakes fall beside a red hot sheet-metal stove.

The snow, the tea.

October 9

Shimun looks at my feet—does she have enough emptiness to walk without thinking for hours on pathways of vertigo, float on the moss, slide on the ice, surprise vibrations in the air, laughter that shines between the folds of the land, at this time when the caribou sings to seduce and the man who hunts it and the female it watches? The fluffy lichens give us springy footsteps. We float among the nomads and the mists on the paths made by old sleds on the trail of the woodland caribou, sometimes a pair of antlers shed during a moult surfaces from the mosses, and we mount it on a shrub the height of the animal's head. You laugh each time you start a story, yes, this man who understood the sound of the female caribou makes you laugh. "No woman wanted to marry him because of his big nose, even though he was a good hunter, that man . . . A female caribou asked him to undress, took a few steps in front of him, and he started walking on all fours, suddenly changing into a caribou. He lived as a caribou." In the course of your story, you become more and more serious, stroking the antlers, you remember word for word the story of the One who had lived as a caribou and of whom no trace had ever been found. "When it came time for the hunt, the men set out to search for him. They were told, Be careful not to kill him! But when all the caribou were dead, he was no longer there, he was already somewhere else . . . " Your fingers follow the curve of the antlers of the young male. "But how did he do it . . . ," your glasses mist up, " . . . to be somewhere else that way? The Kakushapatak called the spirits, and he was there, in the shaking tent, he, Papakassik[u], the Man who had lived as a caribou. It's him, the Master of the Caribou. He's the one we ask for permission to kill the caribou. He's still here, still today."

Through the song of an old man who dreams and makes the bones of the caribou tremble against the skin of the caribou in the drum, the legend has travelled through the territory at the speed of the wind; it is still heard as an echo from Tshishe-shatshit to Pakut-shipit to Ekuanitshit, going from star to dream through wind, from animal to man through dream, and from man to animal through the touch of a sled on the snow.

October 10

Before dawn, Shimun turns the black knob of the radio and he waits, sitting on a log with a cup of tea, for his old friends to wake up on lakes Uauahk, Utukuanhek, Katnukamaht, and Teueikan. The static of the CB radio waves imitates the noise of the embers in the stove. The voices make their way among the spruce needles, the bird nests, the antennas of the antlers, the sparks from shavings, and emerge from the box, as red as the passion of being in movement. Thanks to the radio, we wake up at the same time in the tents that are scattered across Nutshimit. We tell our dreams of the night, talk about the weather, and our plans for the day. The word *kuessipan*, "over to you," punctuates all the conversations, followed by a sparkling silence, our expectation sharpened by the desire for voices from elsewhere. We have a supply of batteries.

October 11

Shimun and Penassin are resting in the camp. I go to set marten traps on the other side of the lake with Nuenau and Shamani. Kimo the wolf dog swims after the canoe. The skeleton of an ancient camp on a big island reminds Nuenau of the first autumn she spent on Lake Kukamessit with her father. "I decided to go with him when my mother left us. I wanted to help him. The school entrusted him with young trainees so he could teach them life in the woods. I was afraid he would get tired. Shimun taught me both the work of women and the work of men: bake home-made bread, carry heavy loads, chop wood, set traps, butcher animals, tan hides . . . " Nuenau lights a fire on the beach. I dry my soaking wet pants. Although I'm a little older than her, Nuenau takes care of me like a child who is not aware of the surrounding dangers. In the same way her ancestors must have taken care of the first arrivals, the Tshishe-Mishtikushuat, Those who arrived in big wooden canoes. They looked after them, dressed them, fed them, guided them. Nomadism requires that you always keep a reserve of the best portion of food for the stranger or the visitor, an ancestral vision of mutual aid. Message sticks still dot Nutshimit, on the beaches, in the forest. The tshissinuatshitakana were planted two by two to alert those who come that way of the abundance or the lack of game. The more the stick was placed at an angle to the support close to the ground, the greater the risk of famine. If on the contrary it was set very high, that meant there was good hunting. Its orientation indicated the direction the clan had taken, like a compass. In all cases, the message sticks were an invitation to sharing.

October 12

The plane comes to pick up Penassin, who has to return to her job as a social worker in the village. She leaves with a heavy heart. Ours are, too, seeing her fly away. We are only four now, Shimun, Nuenau, Shamani, and myself, still connected to this lake, to this mountain, and to this forest until the water freezes, until it snows on the ice, and the ice gets thick enough so that the plane, equipped with skis, can land again.

Shimun, kneeling on his mattress, unfolds the topographical map. Two hunting territories: that of Nuenau and Shamani, that of Shimun and me.

We have the southwest one:
small lake
river
waterfall
river
Kukamessiu-utshu mountain
And the northeast one:
small Lake Kukamess
arm of land
lake
narrow curve
minishtikuss
little island
big Lake Kukamess

Which means: one day go up, the next day come back down, check the traps by criss-crossing the lake by canoe and soon on snowshoes when it's frozen. Every day, leave at dawn, paddling or walking for six to eight hours, come together again in the tent, chop wood, go get water, talk on the CB radio, tell each other stories, laugh, dream. It feels good with the fire in the stove tended by Shimun.

October 13

We cross the lake by canoe. Nuenau teaches me how to shoot the .22 rifle. I aim at a clump of snow at the top of a fir tree.

For the first time, I see an animal caught in a trap, a marten. I look into its eyes for a long time. It's panting to frighten us. It pains me to think that it will die. I have to get used to it—our daily life, from trap to trap.

October 14

Shimun goes back up the river of his origin like a salmon. "My late grandfather was born in Davis Inlet in Labrador. One day he left with his companions to the other side, where he'd never been. He said that they met Innus from Sept-Îles. Those Innus invited them to go there with them. They travelled on foot at first, after by canoe. The Innu from Sept-Îles loaned them two canoes. It was the first time they'd gone down to the St Lawrence. The canoes were small and heavily loaded. My grandfather said that they arrived at the mouth of the Mishtashipu. He remembered it. They went as far as Sept-Îles. It was there he saw the priest for the first time and he became a Catholic. He had no religion before. He was a demon before, ha, ha. He was christened, he confessed, and received his first communion. Everything you want a Catholic to do, eh! That summer, he also married my grandmother. They went to live in Ekuanitshit. Her father's name was Pashin. That's our name today."

October 15

Nuenau teaches me how to skin minks and martens. As you pull the inside-out fur, a liquid that stings your hands oozes from the animal.

October 16

With Shimun, on the trail of a porcupine with oval tracks turned inward. "It must have swum across the river!" We take the canoe. Shimun finds the tracks again and stops, his eyes turned to the sky: "Kak!"

The porcupine has climbed high up in a spruce tree, leaving an ochre trail on the trunk where it chewed the bark. Shimun hands me the rifle. "Aim at the head."

I don't dare shoot. My hands are shaking. I don't want to shoot. I shoot, thinking porcupine is Shimun's favourite meat. The porcupine tumbles into the snow. The animal is still breathing a little. I hit it in the throat. Tears cloud my eyes.

"Shimun, it's not really dead . . . "

"So off to the hospital with the porcupine!"

Shimun pinches the animal's skin where the heart is. He

carries it, the belly against his back, to the canoe. Nuenau will remove its quills with a spatula over a campfire, and tomorrow we will eat it.

October 17

The wind lifted the canvas door all night long. We cut fir branches to replace the old ones on the tent floor and quietly we wash our clothes with water from the lake heated on the stove. A day of rest.

Tonight the wolves are howling. The wolves, when they howl, they give everything, give themselves to water, mountain, forest, man, wind, keeping only the starry thread of the song where the instinct for life vibrates. I feel only one danger, the danger of loving someone as deeply outside and inside as the wolf when it's howling. Would my heart survive this confession spoken in a single sound, a single breath, a single cry?

October 18

We spend another day on all the water of the lakes, with the sea like an absent presence in the wind. The island is my thrill, landscape that put to bed my childhood on the horizon. I am old of the sea and young of the land. Here I have to relearn to look, to hold things, to walk.

The lake island is not the sea island. The lake island is animal, full of life that abounds there now. Through the trees that embrace it, it stretches to the land and stretches to the sky. The sea island is a hollow of rock and sky that touch each other like two hands, leaving a void where the winds blow in and where all the returnings, all the departures meet. The sea island is a call, an absolute escape.

With a vague feeling of salt on my lips, I paddle more intensely on Shimun's lake, I look for birds, reaching always higher with my gaze.

October 19

Shimun: "I came into the world somewhere in the territory. When a child came into the world, I was told, a child had been found in a dry tree stump. I believed what they told me, and so I was afraid of tree stumps. I was afraid of finding a baby!"

How could I have found greater protection than yours? In Nutshimit, you were born. You are the body of the forest.

October 20

They are as old as snowfalls, the footprints left by a moccasin. The wind mixes them with those of the animals so that a man like Shimun dreams, stands up, walks, hunts as if the ground, the sky were his skin.

The most ancient tracks are also the softest. A bit of bark cut in the trunk of a tree in memory of a direction, a mark left in passing on Shimun's cheek.

October 21

As if I were waking up after a long nighttime journey, during which I let myself be led by someone else, I realize only now where I have arrived—in the forest, on the shore of a lake where the snow is falling.

Here, life is gentler than a dream and yet more real than any moment I've ever lived. Look, walk, chop down a tree, carry wood, draw water from the lake, skin an animal, laugh, relax, make bread, love everything around us.

October 22

Long necklaces circle our legs, bones of the heads of lake trout in the shape of silhouettes. Whole families dance in groups in the skull of the fish and spin on the ground of our dreams. We will have good fishing tomorrow at Pikuanipanan.

October 23

Nishuasht kukamessat.
Seven lake trout.

October 24

The lake freezes starting at its heart. The canoe season is over. The sky appears even more immense. Nuenau, Shamani, and I set out on snowshoes as far as the waterfall. We follow the tracks of partridges, little backwards arrow points. Great silences spread out in front of us. Our eyes move back and forth between the ground and the fir tree branches. We walk, suspended between two waters.

Tonight the dogs are thinking of us. They are barking at the lake. What's going by? A marten? A fox? The reflection of a star?

October 25

Atop spruce trees
the porcupines are swinging
lanterns of the sun.

   Reconnect with Nordic memory. Follow the trail of an animal, kill an animal, eat it, breath within the immensity. I try to give in to this new relationship with nature but, in fact, I don't have to take off many skins to find the desire to hunt. It is just there, in the muscles and in a most secret place that has to do with love.

October 26

Rain. We stay in the tent. We listen to the lives of other lakes on the radio. I dream, letting myself be cradled by the deep voices. "Kukamessit . . . Kukamessit . . . Shimuniss . . . Little Simon . . . Tshipeten a?

   "Eshe nipeten . . . Kuessipan!"

   "Nuapamati atiku, mishishtu, mamatsheshkaneu. Patetat pineuat ninipauat. Kuessipan!" A large caribou with big antlers has been spotted close to Lake Katnukamaht. They have caught five partridges.

   Just as the wind shaped its caresses on the mountains, the ground, and the sky, those two forces, ultimately distant, have come to an agreement. The mountains have come close to the sky, magnetized by a gentle origin. The stars have imprinted the night. The silence has become matter. There was only sound, the quivering of a wave on the instinctive path. The stone has understood the secret; it has forgiven the soul for moving into the infinite and asked the ground to embrace its life so that the murmur of the stars flows into its skin. Since then, the transparency of the sky burns with it.

October 27

The lake has thawed a bit. It seems to be enough for us to set out by canoe. I marvel at all the textures that the lake can take on. Where it's a little icy, it turns milky and the trees are reflected in a stippled haze. In other places, ice has thickened, hard, cutting; we have to break it by smashing the paddles through it repeatedly to clear a passage. Elsewhere still, tiles of ice are layered on the lake in a range of soft greys. Shimun admits that it is dangerous to navigate. A thin layer of ice covers the hull. It would be easy to capsize when we encounter frozen water. At the portage, we slide the canoe over the snow. The dog Tushis gets caught in the otter trap, that little nut . . . Always the mist. We paddle in a gradation of black and white. I shoot at ducks and a muskrat, and I miss. I know I'm shooting reluctantly. I have no desire to kill, but a great desire to look at the world with Shimun. All the greys of the world are here, from matte to silver, from mica to quartz. The wind comes by sometimes with secrets. I hear it talk of love like a smile.

October 28

Snow and wind. A thick breeze is passing by the shore of the lake. Heavy wind arising between the land, the air, and the water. Coming close in silence, feet in the moss, and feeling the emotion of things that are changing into spirit. They blend with each other and become that rustling of burning air that undresses you in spite of the layers of clothes. An inner confidence penetrates you, the joy of a present that rises from the crumbly strata of the shore and the footprints of those who have walked it before you. Even an animal. A wind. The fall of fruit. Just a thought that would stretch out there, on the shore of the lake. An openwork in the consciousness of the world. The fresh pain of being alive this morning. Get up, eyes creased with dream. And want to shout all the love that makes you carry the land with its perilous beauty.

October 29

I never have martens in my traps. When I set them, I warn the martens not to get caught in them. I don't have the courage to kill them by pinching their hearts with my hand.

On a trail dug more deeply than the others, Shimun recognizes the signs of caribou passing. The trail goes back to September. They left towards the northwest. "Look, the caribou have scraped their antlers on these bushes!"

October 30

Chopped down trees, carried, sawed, stacked the wood. In the tent, with Nuenau, we embroider a sun, a tree, a porcupine on our canvas bags. Through the simplicity of brief instants, I relearn the world by hand. A quiet, relaxed day. I dream with a smile that comes from later.

It's snowing in the deepest dreams of my existence.

There are a thousand and one ways to listen to the sea.

There are a thousand and one ways to listen to snow falling.

October 31

We put the canoe in the water in the powerful night. You hold the stern of the boat while I step inside, leaning on the gunwales that still smell of filler. Dry noise of the paddle against the bottom ribs of the hull. Damp aroma of your loose tobacco mixed with the acid smell of the marten glands in a transparent bag. Sparks glow outside the stove pipe sticking through the roof of the tent on the shore. I sit down in the position of the puller in front and you, in that of the skipper. "We're going that way!" Your right hand splitting the East and the North in one movement. We will head towards the big lake, a little ocean in the midst of the frozen lands. We will spend another beautiful day together in the heart of your world. It will beat intensely. You will stroke its cracked skin with the palm of your canoe.

The Autumn Moon

November 1

The sky scatters into snow dust. The waves break towards the canoe.

November 2

Mist shines at dawn. The sun seems to be coming back. The lake has become a mirror. Everything is precise and clear above as well as below.

November 3

The humans are dreaming a lot and the birds too. Maybe the dreams of three partridges, Nuenau's dreams and mine, were the same last night . . .

> The silence covers the footsteps
> of the birds
> and the tracks come down

from the height of the branches
like pieces of heaven
the partridge.

Shimun and Shamani smile when they see us coming back with our three catches, and we in their eyes are as proud as children. We pluck the partridges, while they're still warm, on the shore of the lake. Nuenau asks me to close my eyes like her. "You feel the wind?"

November 4

Canoe. Lac du Nord, lake of the north.

We prepare the partridges killed yesterday to make leather. When the knife cuts the translucent skin of the throats, spruce and fir needles spill out.

November 5

It's cold, minus thirty according to Shimun. The lake froze during the night. Before walking on the ice, we have to wait for it to be at least five centimetres thick. The heart of the lake is a mirror with sparkling outlines. A band of spruce trees is reflected in the last lagoons. We walk as far as the waterfall, in snowshoes along the shore. Paddles in our hands, we scatter the frosty powder on the frozen shores of the lake to help us distinguish the water from the land under our feet. The wolf maikan has left deep tracks on that same path. It must be big and heavy. It went past the camp.

That evening, when I go get water from the lake, the long

whistle of a rifle bullet crosses from one shore to another. I look in vain for the invisible hunter. "That's normal, it's the ice singing as it forms. Sometimes it sounds like a rifle shot, but you'll see, the nights when it's very cold, it's even more beautiful," Nuenau explains while we're playing "Indian cards" and Shimun takes the opportunity to cheat.

November 6

Penassin calls us on the radio. I've received a package. She'd really like to open it. I'm curious too. It's *L'Étoile polaire* (the Pole Star), a poetry collection by Yvon Le Men. I lose her voice in the static, but the lines that reach me seem so close to what we are experiencing here that I can barely believe it . . .

> At the northern extreme of the world
> there is a country
> too small
> to appear on the globe
> too remote
> not to have to live on its own
>
> . . .
>
> The man goes to his brother through the wolf
> the sled to the fire through the snow
> the guide with the woman singer through the dog

Shimun says that before the voices came from dreams. They didn't need the radio. In a group there was always a woman or a man who could communicate with those who were far away.

The red box, the sounds of which lull us in the evening and wake us gently before dawn, seems to me like the receptacle for the dreams of the body of the forests.

November 7

Hearing ice sing is not of this world. It's the sound of the depths of the sky meeting the sound of the depths of the land. The song rises from the water in a translucent sheet and comes down again, ice on the forest. Under the tent, that night, the four of us listen together . . .

> The ice
> when it forms
> sings
> of the owl
> and the whale
> in its throat
> an echo to the stars.
> What is human in us breaks away from us.

November 8

For two days, we travel the lakes in moccasins, on ice as hard as life—if you think about anything else, you fall. We set out when the fuchsia flower of dawn opens on the mountain Tushis-ushakatikum. The ice is still black with night. Shimun trots along, glowing. He is free to go everywhere from lake to lake, from island to island, from trap to trap, a wooden shovel in his left hand to test the thickness of the ice by sound, an axe in his right hand to clear a path in the mountain. The little dog Tushis jumps, slides, leaps in the air. I am slowly mastering our new world. "Don't look at your feet, keep your eyes on the tops of the fir trees in the distance, where the sky touches the land, that is where we find courage." A smile extends Shimun's eyes as if to stretch the horizon across his face. Shimun knows how to read the ice from a distance. When he feels that it may break, he signals me to change my path. I am overwhelmed by this mineral world that brings us closer to the infinite. Pastel blue, carpeted with slightly pink stars of frost at the beginning of dawn, ice becomes, as day breaks, black under the slate domed sky. Transparent, it reveals the fish swimming beneath our feet. The islands seem to rise a little closer to the sky like perfectly round stories.

Behind each forest hides a lake. Shimun takes me farther than usual. He is looking for the beaver lodge, but finds only old dams—each year, the beavers move. Feeling dizzy, Shimun sits down on a rock. He asks me for sugar. I have no more landmarks, not even a mountain. If he were to pass out, I wouldn't be able to go get help at the camp. The lumps of sugar I find in his game bag give him a bit of energy again, but I'm worried— he often complains of headaches.

November 9

The wind blows strongly over the powdery snow that covers the ice. Big white streaks fray on the black.

November 10

Solitude is looking at the self. It does not exist. Life of the fir tree, life of the beaver, life of the cloud: all in us. Here, something is stronger than death. Destiny is just the coming day. Tomorrow, we will get up at five. Shimun will relight the fire in the stove. He will talk to his friends, Antoine and Charles, who wake up in other tents, on the shores of other lakes. They will update each other on the weather and their hunting plans for the day. Antoine mostly hunts beaver. He lives on bannock, tea, and beaver. The tea will be hot in the metal teapot on the stove. We will eat partridge, caribou, or else bacon and eggs, if there are any left in the provisions. We will set out when the red of dawn emerges from the black. The ice will cry out everywhere. I will put the .22 over my shoulder and the game bag on my back, held with a cord across my chest, snowshoes on my feet. Shimun will carry the axe and the shovel. In his bag, he will put matches, a few traps, pieces of trout as bait for the martens, a pan, two cups, and packets of powdered chocolate. We will walk, we will walk, we will walk: lake, forest, lake, mountain, lake, island, river, waterfall, lake. We will maybe set a snare for the white hare, if we see its crazy tracks. As Shimun says: "The hares are always drunk, their tracks go every which way . . . "

November 11

Powdery weather. The river trembles between the lakes flayed by the cold. Its body is a bottomless movement. We see solitary days of walking without leaving tracks. They contemplate before offering their new page to those who will cross them.

We give our footsteps the tempo of heavy flakes. Hare paws have the power of a soft faded fur warming our frozen fingers in the canvas pouch where the .22 bullets roll, those hollows devouring my hand. The animal feels it can become the dream of an animal.

With the first dream of the world, the Bear is breathing. He understands silence in its emptiness. The maternity of the land is in the Bear, who is the father. He growls. He points to the sky. When he breathes, he drinks the wind. The Bear is where the silence breaks. He breathes out. The wind scatters like a dream of mother-of-pearl on the surface of everything that, then, comes to life.

November 12

Snowshoe tracks on the white river. A path for two. Shimun's smile and my smile, because time has written to us that it won't go by without telling us. We are connected by an incongruous friendship, an old man and a young woman.

From tundra to taiga, going past the black spruce of the sub-arctic forest, Shimun's life extends from Natuashish in Labrador to Ekuanitshit on the shores of the Gulf of St Lawrence. If I knew how to read palm lines, I would read Shimun's straight from the land that, from north to south, and from east to west, remembers his footsteps and those of his mother, Maniten. I would say that the world was created in the image of their eyes, maps painted according to the winds: land, courage, sky, love, water, respect, fire.

The other day, Shimun let me go alone, onto the big lake, to check a hare snare. He returned before me to the camp. I wasn't afraid of losing my way back, which I knew by heart. But I had an uneasy feeling. I often looked over my shoulder as if the whole forest was watching me with astonishment, slight reproach but benevolence. I walked on the big lake between the islands, found the snare, which was empty, went around the forest, crossed another lake, past the portage to check out the otter trap. When I got back to the camp, just before nightfall, I was stunned by the immensity become dizzying without my walking companion, my landmark—the tree, rock, beaver man. I immediately saw in his eyes the worry that my three hours of solitary walking had brought him. Then, and as often happens in the evening, we laughed a lot. He told me about the relief he felt hearing from a distance the snow cracking under my snowshoes. That day I understood how much my happiness in being here is connected to Shimun. When we set out on his hunting territory, it's through his eyes that I see, through his smile that I smile, through his serenity that I feel fulfilled, through his hunger that I hunt, through his respect for the animal that I shoot. How could I ever measure the gift that Shimun has given me by inviting me to walk in him?

November 13

The wind

restless

white

Under the mist cleared by a bundle of moss, the nomads clinging to the deer by their antlers fly from body to body, jostling between breaths to the north of autumn, turning colours and footsteps upside down. Walk, small joy of the last fruits to be gathered, my lucky star between the branches. Do you remember that wooden cup hanging from a pole in the tent? Snow, gust, storm, ice, thaw, frost. Your face attached to the shape of a lake by your lips.

The nomads pour glasses of breath into the bowls hanging from the trees, an old language of Nutshimit both soft and rough. The stretched marten skins burst our sleep with each wolf howl. Strange confused partridges under a sheet of boreal needles of which our tongues retain the scent less sweet than the beaver meat taking care of our lungs.

November 14

But where is the beaver lodge? The four of us are heading to the big lake. We're still learning something from the sky passing under the dawn. The ice is pale blue, the light, strong and fresh. We go to the stream, three hours' walk from the camp, on the bank where Shimun had found a piece of wood cut down by a beaver's teeth in the month of October. It's here, the stick-and-mud lodge of the beavers, at the end of the stream, as tall as two men, the entrance under the water. Shimun and Shamani break through the ice to sink a trap.

When the blankets weigh down with fatigue, it's reassuring for us to know that the stars are lighting lamps on the snow. We whisper stories that brush the flames of the candles wedged in the fir-bough carpet, between our mattresses. Shimun nicknames me Amishku-ishkueu, Beaver Woman. In the time when the animals talked, a hunter had fallen in love with a female beaver. He got up every day before dawn to try to see her red fur flowing through the waterfalls of the river. The female beaver sensed the human's feelings towards her and invited him to come live with her. "But she made sure to tell him, don't take off your mittens, you'll need webbed paws to swim like me." Before that day, humans didn't swim. They only moved by canoe on the water. "Follow me, do like me . . . " The human let himself be guided by love. As his body submerged, his feet and his hands became webbed, his hairless skin became dressed in gleaming fur. He was happy to look more like the one who had conquered his soul. She taught him the ways of beavers under the water and on the land. He revealed to her the hunting tricks of the humans. Today, the beavers thwart those tricks. Amishku-ishkueu is the origin of an alliance between animals and humans.

November 15

The stars have given memory to the wind. But where do the legends come from? From the light that falls from the stars in the wind? Each star is the mother of an animal returning to slumber in her. Our tracks have disappeared. New borders— trail of a wolf, of an otter—outline the map of the lake.

November 16

Snow sky
at the end of the stream
Shimun caught a beaver
in his trap
animal of land and water
strong within
the world.

But the dog Kimo refuses to pull the sled where the beaver has been laid. Nuenau takes it on her back. I relieve her and carry it on my back. Shimun gets angry, says we don't know how to carry it. He ties it his way. I steal it from him, he takes it back from me. In the evening, we laugh: what's the point of arguing on a big lake about carrying a beaver!

November 17

Heavy, wet body of the beaver, night fur on shoulders determined to take the animal back to the camp. Between the skin and the fat, your hands teach me to insert the hooked knife with a quick movement of the wrist. Sitting in your old navy-blue sweatpants worn at the knees, you did not want to spend the autumn in a house on the seashore, preferring the Nutshimit of your birth.

You never exhaust a face. There always remains a crease at the corner of the lips, a sheen in the eye that hasn't been seen. I see something else of you when I think of your mother, Maniten, of her strange little eyes that roll, keeping well oiled the will to see beyond the slope. She brought you into the world along the way—she, and all her grandmothers with her. Knowing that a church was waiting for your baptism on the seashore, she plunged through Nutshimit, pulling a sled on which you glided, swaddled among your brothers and sisters.

Maniten insisted we go to the north with our feet nice and warm in the woollen socks she knitted for us. She taught me how to embroider beads on a piece of leather which she had cut in the shape of a foot. She guided the needle I was holding with her hand with nods of her head and a skeptical look on her face. "I've seen everything, I know the whole of Nutshimit, but I don't want to go back there anymore. I'd miss my old travelling companions too much."

You inherited from her that tender gaze watching for the least excuse to laugh at the movements of another. With Nuenau and Penassin, who play tricks on me—"Thank our grandmother for the good meal of dried meat . . . "—I sometimes spoke to Maniten repeating to her naively funny phrases in Innu-aimun. I'll never forget that the word for "dried meat" is *pashteu-uiash* and not *passikan*, "gun". Maniten pretended to be serious, then she burst out with a clear laugh before adding her own two cents' worth to the joke by congratulating me on my luck in having tasted that food. We laughed helplessly all three of us, her granddaughters and I, at her ancient humour. If she hears me talk on the radio now, she must raise an eyebrow, hesitating between amusement and disapproval—I half trust Nuenau when she asks me to call old Antoine at Lake Uauahk using his supposed nickname Massenitak. And how upset is she going to get when she learns that Nuenau secretly sewed the legs of my pyjamas, half an inch a day, until I think I've gotten so fat I can't put them on anymore . . . We can fall asleep roaring with laughter. If there was a prize for making jokes, we know who would win it.

November 18

A long streak of silvery sun moves across the surface of the lake. You teach me the names of the mountains.

> Tushis-ushakatikum
> The mountain where there are always caribou for
>   Tushis
> Kukamessiu-utshu
> The mountain of the lake trout

When you name them, pointing them out with a hand gesture leaded with the colour of your eyes, you imprint life in me. We share now, more than a memory, a piece of your path. Walking without making noise, taking a little food and setting out again, leaving the animals time to reproduce. You sing the book of the land begun by your ancestors, which did not impose on places a single name forever. They waited for an event to renew the names along the way. "One day, two old women went in a canoe to cast their net on a lake, so they called that lake the Place where the old women will cast their net."

November 19

"Naur, ishkuteu mishau minashkuat!" You have fun with the idea that we are lighting again "a big fire in the woods!" The time before, I burned my snow pants. "Naur . . . " You liked seeing me fixing the holes with pieces of tent canvas.

> In Innu-aimun
> the L is pronounced N
>
> you call me Nord
> you make me melt.

November 20

You chop off dry tree branches with your axe and you push them into the snow to hold the pot over the fire. You sprinkle chocolate from a bag into a cup of hot water that you then hand to me. You remind me of my grandfather Robert who would make me big glasses of blood-orange juice in the morning. His eyeglasses had the same shape as yours. You haven't experienced the same wars, but you have the same silences between your lips, and in your eyes the subdued light of the horizon between two sunny spells, the wry smile of the resistance fighters. My grandfather loved to play dominos, smoke Gitanes, buy me pretty dresses. He said he had found me in a rose, not in a tree stump. I followed him as I do you who are teaching me to walk again and keep upright on the ice. I follow you in Nutshimit with my eyes closed. My grandfather gave me his eyes as the key to enter the horizon. The world we walk as adults unfolds from a little handkerchief with embroidered initials carried by our grandfathers in the inside pocket of their raincoats smelling of lavender, tobacco, and anise.

November 21

Nuenau, Shamani, and I return to the beaver lodge. Shimun stays at the camp to chop wood and listen to cassettes of country music while he cooks.

Our skin bronzed by the dawn, we plunge into a crystal—ice has formed around all the needles of all the black spruces, all the fir trees, and makes them transparent against the light. But when we look at the trees, with our backs to the sun, they appear ashen against the chalk-blue sky.

Female of the beaver.

November 22

Each in turn, we pull the sled strapped to our hips to bring back to camp the logs chopped by Shimun in the forest. I had never seen myself this way: the importance of hands, eyes, shoulders, back, belly, hips, thighs, feet, all united in the act of finding something to eat, to drink, to warm ourselves.

November 23

The paths extend across the lake, those of the sled, the snowshoes, the moccasins, the dog paws. The animals have made me love their absence. When someone is walking on their trail, desire grows with fatigue, and the more desire grows, the wider the gaze.

The wind is secret like a ritual: love, strength, calm, love.

November 24

In this country where everything is white, lake, forest, mountain, hunter's coat, I love the colour that our life takes on. When
we get up ahead of the dawn of the lake, the dawn of the dog,
the dawn of the snow, we say nothing. But the red that the cold
paints on our faces, the pricks of light that the sun drives into
our eyes, the weight of the axe in our arms breaking the ice to
draw water, thank the dawn instead of the words you could say.

Silence is a prayer that extends high and far.

November 25

The whiteness connects us to each other. We follow the paths
in the snow to eat together. We chop down dry trees to warm
ourselves together. We have a dog and a white tent for four.
Humanity is the three others. Yesterday, when you wanted to
kill Kimo, I grabbed your arm in midair before you threw the
axe. You explained to me that it wasn't doing its dog's work.
That it refused to pull the little sled. You told me you'd killed
lots of dogs in your lifetime. And you laughed when I told
you that Kimo was my friend. "It's not your friend, it's just a
dog." It's true that I didn't want it to die. But I had another
fear . . . That Shamani would resent you for killing his dog and
that our little island of humanity would become unlivable for
the time we have left to spend on Kukamessit. Your eyes, when
I stopped your arm, reflected the spark of friction, my land, my
customs, my beliefs confronting yours in slow motion; euphoria
and fear were mixed in those few seconds when I put myself

between you and the dog, carnal contact between life and death, the brief flash of the axe that veers from its path, the dog that flattens its ears and moves away, runs away from us, leaves us to our fight of an old man and a little girl from two continents, and even though I looked ridiculous expressing my feelings for the animal, I will always remember the choreography of our bodies on that lake, your tender smile when I forced the flow of tears to move you, your laugh to wipe away the emotion, to take back your role as a nomad hunter obeying laws of survival, your questioning that has been seen—and what if she really felt friendship for that dog, and if we were, in spite of our differences, two fellow-travellers liberated from their principles by the possibility of laughter—Shimun, and your fading season-blue fleece jacket, Shimun, and your snow name abandoned to the wind, Shimun.

November 26

A storm covers us. The snow has taken possession of all the branches of all the fir trees. The morning pushes us to sleep. As on a boat, we take shifts. When I wake up, I embroider, on the canvas sack in which I put my bullets, a moon of white beads, punctuated with two blue beads. I surround it with a beaver tooth and with a porcupine tooth, smaller, both red.

Kimo moans like a wolf in love on the shore of the lake. Who knows if a she-wolf is trying to seduce him?

The wind blows strongly through the branches of the spruce trees. That wind smells of the earth.

November 27

Tshitshue minushkueuipan
tshitshue minushkueuipan

truly, she was a beautiful woman
truly, she was a beautiful woman

ueshausham massenitakushinua utauassima
ueshausham matshishishinua utauassima

oh her child is so cute
oh her child is so ugly

you dance in the middle of the lake your feet
strike the ice

you laugh she is so beautiful that woman
he was a cutie her child

this breath in you the trees
in your little man body dancing
with his paddle on the powdery snow.

A big caribou makes you skip, jump. He's with you, of course,
The one of which no tracks have ever been found . . . That
beautiful set of antlers that form your laugh, your hair tousled,
your river raging under the ice and the next waterfall to climb,
a dream rippling around your shoulders, the mountain for horizon and the smell of fire for hope.

November 28

Nice and warm in the hollow of the lake trout's belly, you teach me to read the damp snow wind on my skin, to stroke the ice with the soles of my feet until I feel the cave where the nomads hear the breathing of the drum. Everything is white except our silhouettes. Are we dreams? Is it you who dream me or I who rolled myself up in a ball under your coat, to follow your copper wrinkles in your full-moon face lighting up the skin of Grandmother Lake Trout?

November 29

At night, the nomads visit us under the blankets with animal patterns, camouflage of wolves. The night beads in forests trembling at the tips of candles. We are forests for the breeze gently drawing on our foreheads lakes, routes, our wrinkles in which the reflection of the day takes on hues of an astounding purple.

It is so tawny, the light of dawn, that it chases away our tracks. We passed that way, but nothing says so. We have become something between animal and wind.

November 30

I didn't know that happiness was an old sheet-metal stove, a lit candle, a pair of snowshoes, a paddle, some canvas. You tell me the legends you learned from your grandparents who themselves learned them from the time when the animals talked. The wolves follow the caribou. I follow you.

The Little Moon

December 1

Everything was white as a sheet of paper, but for a little while, something shines faintly. The golden colour permeates the sky and the silvery ice like a promise.

December 2

This morning it's very cold. Shimun lifts his snowshoes very high. The fresh snow flies away. There are flashes in the mist. When we get to the big lake, clouds leave behind snowfalls. The orange and saffron rise on our backs. The cold carves in the lake a multitude of waves breaking on the islands. Shimun lights a big fire on a beach. I break a layer of ice to fill the little pot. I hand it to Shimun. He hangs the handle on a branch, above the flames. From his game bag, he takes out two tea bags which he throws into the simmering water. We know that soon the plane will come to pick us up. These days should never end. The sun swallows the last tinges of dawn. But the water in the pot turns amber.

December 3

I carry a mischievous happiness with me. I think, "I love you," without knowing who that feeling is directed to. With each second rises in me the first breath of a desire.

The world has flesh, a heart.

Fire

It's only under a fire rock
sheltered from a cold and solitary winter
that I heard the heartbeats of the land
and it's there that I learned to listen.

RITA MESTOKOSHO

Riding the Clouds

Shiship-pishim[u], the moon of the return of the waterfowl
April 2006

My hand trembles brushing the globe. A beach of pollen borders its blues. It closes up, all against the land, the wind rose.

The wind undoes its canvas in the home of the dawn before spreading its currents in all directions. Sea, Heaven, Earth, Fire, East, South, West, North. We choose a destination for ourselves, but the weave is so tight that we cannot avoid the forces intersecting it. The adventure of the tireless wind keeps life in movement. It urges us to write with the tracks that we leave on the land, through the gazes of will that we imprint on the horizon. We leave from the centre and move off to join the edge of the canvas in the space of a lifetime. Sometimes we come back to the centre, when we are born, when we fall, when we love, when we feel the light, when we die.

I was in Ekuanitshit a week before cancer finally took from Shimun what remained of his weight. He became very light while his eyes took on the poise of the mountain. It was December 1999. I believe that he must not have felt any affinity with the third millennium. I slipped away to leave him with his children. As usual I left kissing him on both cheeks.

We promised each other we'd meet again in the spring for the arrival of the geese, without really understanding what it meant to see each other again if he were dead, because both of us knew he only had a few days left to live. When I was flying over the North Shore in an airplane, Shimun was flying too. He was going back to his hunting territory on the antlers of a very old caribou.

We met in the air that morning, but it wasn't the last time. We did see each other again, as planned, one spring. Labrador rippled the tawny ochre of its old hills and shed its mossy coat in handfuls of lakes. They announced the start of a romantic movie. The flight attendant asked me to lower my window shade to facilitate viewing. With headphones on my ears, my eyes riveted to the small screen, I must have had the same blissful smile as my neighbour to the right. I dozed quietly. And then, it was just too much. I raised the shade in spite of the instructions. I leaned towards the window. I recognized the shape of that lake, thought I was hallucinating. We were flying over the only lake whose shape I was really familiar with among the thousands that the Quebec-Labrador peninsula is awash in, Kukamess-nipi. I had walked on that water when it was frozen. That was where we'd set up our camp! I would have liked to shout to all the passengers so they would stop watching *Long Island Love Story* and contemplate with me the uterine shape of the lake of my friend Shimun. With my hands pressed against the glass of the window, I recognized the rounded peak of the mountain called Tushis a bit to the south and soon after the Saint-Jean River hurtling towards the salt water.

Seeing me come back according to plan in the spring among the migrating geese, Shimun rose high above his territory. He discreetly slipped onto the airplane with his mischievous smile. Using I don't know what trick he pulled from his game bag, he roused me from my drowsiness to allow me to revisit the place where I had loved being with him so much. It's almost as if he's replaced my plastic cup with his little pot of good strong sweet tea. I thought I heard him say: "Shash eieshkusteu tshitshue nipishapui! The real tea is ready! Apu uikat nipishapui anite upashtimakanit! The tea is bad on airplanes." A hint of melancholy was diluted in my sense of fulfilment.

Now that I'm a mother, I feel more strongly the concerns of my Innu sisters about what could happen to their children. The landmarks bequeathed by the Elders disappear with them. Not one year has gone by without me returning to Ekuanitshit. Since the birth of my son, a new emotion has appeared in the eyes of Nuenau and Penassin, a sense of relief. Raphaël learned his first word in Innu-aimun, "kakuss" "little porcupine," babbling with Tshiuetin and Maniu, Shimun's great-grandsons. He ate his first piece of caribou. It was Maniu, barely one and a half years old, who set down his plate beside Raphaël and shared his meal with him, as Shimun had done with me.

Mishta-Meshkanau, the Highway, the 138

*Ushkau-pishim^u, the moon when the male caribou
rub their antlers to get rid of the velvet*

September 2010

The lightness like a wave follows us to take us back to the
rare places of this land where, at least once, we were happy.
I dreamed it was snowing in Nutshimit. The old name from
dreams, written behind life, continues to demand its share of
existence, whether I hear it or not, it whispers its ancient letters
in my eyes, in my mouth.

Go along the horizon, follow the St Lawrence to the sea,
get fog glitter on our cheeks, always wondering why when it's
misty that we become the most conscious of the light and of
the constellation of fragrances—the salt, the fir tree, the shikuteua, the mosses of lichen, the Labrador tea, the spruce boughs,
the salmon, the sand, the taste of the route in the transparency
of the peninsulas. Take roller-coaster rides on the 138 and meet
again there on foot, hitchhiking, by car, truck, snowmobile,
pickup, airplane, bus, by *Nordik Express*, by dream, by project, in
memory, journey, desire, regret, weeping, joy, love, quest, escape,
friendship, mourning, wandering, ecstasy, pilgrimage.

The storms were not horses. The cows had no collars. We had the scent of the dogs, the transparent voice of the whales, the chlorophyll vision. We were catalysts of clouds, transmitters of pollen, capable of answering from one end of the world to another the calls of those who needed us. Words are magic. You think them and they appear. We have our instinct in hand. They call us travellers, wanderers, emigrants, displaced people, tourists, poets, politicians, navigators, astronauts, alterglobalists, immigrants, explorers. In no time at all, we can be located everywhere on and around the planet. But how many thoughts circulate secretly with the same power as knives and caresses in the air? We take pictures of the marine mammals with our smart phones and we rush to share those images with as many people as possible so that the world knows that we have witnessed the appearance of an endangered species. The trees weep and pray for us to bring them infrared glasses. For us to remember our languages of boxwood, laurel, sage, white spruce, ayahuasca, beech. And if the cows are watching us with that sorry insistence, it's because they are still waiting for us to recognize them as the worthy descendants of aurochs. We are nomads. We plunge through the sea mist. "Whales or refund, nothing to lose." They dressed us like cosmonauts in spite of the heat wave. We climbed into that minibus already almost full to go down to the pier less than a hundred metres away. For an instant, I thought I was in an airport shuttle. It's that subtle background sound of talking where everyone acts as if there was nothing extraordinary about going to rub against the tail of a humpback whale. We are tourists who are going to see the whales on the

St Lawrence River. It's straightforward, plain and simple, everyone in the zodiac. I love feeling like a tourist who is going to see the whales in the Tadoussac area. The storms are not horses. The cows have no collars. There are no sages, soothsayers, shamans, druids, or saints. We are nomads. I saw the Earth move, on a clear day. The blue whale slowly raises its back.

I found myself one evening in Sept-Îles in the company of two travellers I'd met on the bus. With my two chance travel companions, a Haitian man and a German woman, I searched for a place to sleep in that city, but since it was a holiday, people in the convenience stores on the big boulevard did not seem to feel like giving us information, so we walked down to the harbour. I remember the beach, the diamonds, the seagulls, and the mandolins, it was so dark, the flashes from construction sites on the other side of the bay, where nothing can arise but the force of a fire, we walked on the embankment with waves in our souls and our feet poorly shod for a country where the only smiles come from Arnaud Street, since there spurt the sprays, the seagulls, the lighthouse flashes and reflections of containers on the windows of the Hôtel Sept-Îles, a labyrinth of metal rooms with a view of the sea, we resolved to sleep there so as not to be subjected to the sullenness of the people on Laure Boulevard on Thanksgiving weekend, the hotel on the street that begins with an A had airs of blue follies with its undulating nude dancers, soft, violent waves driven into the gulf from the Atlantic which was instinctively made to begin in Newfoundland, where our ancestors went to fish cod, at least that's what we imagined, because how else could they have looked like wounded warriors of the ice floes, those slender gannet eyes, those fingers raw with cold, those smiles of purple legends that populated our childhoods behind the heavy furniture, nicely polished on Sundays, with yellowed lace the colour of apple cider, in the abandoned garages with dip nets and nautical charts with suspect names of fantastic animals—nothing to make us feel like staying or really whet our appetites for the open sea, these are the stories we tell ourselves when we start to tire of journeys and we invent for ourselves the failed fates of merchant sailors, explorers, or pirate brides disappointed by the cheap buccaneers whose charms we fell for without believing too much in their treasures, we got caught up in the game of the Americas just as we get caught up in the greenish net of boreal dawns bathing among the seagulls in the night, without even wondering why they're swimming at this hour, what are they waiting for, stealing each other's places on a saltwater chessboard full of snow crabs and dreams washed up on the banks of Arnaud Street, on Thanksgiving Day, when the absence of work makes faces jaded, heartsick in fact with not knowing how to occupy their bodies in the city laid out according to the letters of the alphabet; we turn around at the end of the embankment brushing against the line of a Thanksgiving Monday fisherman whose activity seemed to us as fruitless as that of the seagulls swimming in the neon green glint of boreal dawns. Our coats were coming unstitched from the inside, night searching in us our last resistance to giving thanks for being alive in spite of the impossibility of knowing where we would be led by those signs of seagulls stolen from the paradise of angels, we only wanted to occupy a room with a view of the sea in the Hôtel Sept-Îles, whatever our origins, our destinations, it was our only desire that evening, we were so different and alike in our endeavours as tattered travellers, our purple or blue scarves, our hopes of vibrating with the night on a great chessboard of which we did not know the most secret laws. A seagull followed us, bringing back in its feathers the hidden light, swam, its webbed feet gliding, felt the currents slide from fjords of the Saguenay to those of Cape Horn, the three-masted model ships zigzagging below the fiftieth parallel, it remembered, the seagull our beacon stopped time, folded the maps until the south and north latitudes coincided, the beginning of the twentieth and twenty-first centuries, located the ancestors who made us mist mantles on the embankment—it's not every day that we hear people refer to their childhood memories under the capes of sailors who let them rise up in the skirts of mistresses—and we were happy, thanks to that seagull escaping from the constellation of its kind, we knew that a grandfather opened for us the path of the water and the land with his mischievous laugh and his Sept-Îles dawn eyes. We walked at the pace of the swimming seagull, feet folded, eyes turned sideways, hands in our pockets and our noses a bit in the air, as the seagulls do when they look at us discreetly; the only thing that counted was that invisible wave of love on which we were surfing with the grandfather bird. We weren't even thinking anymore about that hotel with a view of the sea, near the fish store on Arnaud Street, we were thinking only about sponging from our hearts their elation against driftwood, about bursts of laughter between two big gushes of spray, filled with a sadness the bubbles of which had all burst to change into joy. Even our shoes, too thin for the month of October on the Côte-Nord, seemed to us to be appropriate for the hesitation of our footsteps. We were all set to confront Laure Boulevard with its garages and its video-poker machine bars, with its hotels and its strip malls, its flashing signs and its holiday emptiness, its deserted brick office buildings, its 4x4s prowling in search of a self-service gas station, we walked in zigzags as if we were drunk, the seagulls hanging on our coat-tails. Seven islands, a seagull, and we walked aimlessly in the city on Thanksgiving evening and, seeing that the liquid stars had changed into anemone gelatin in the mist that swelled the bay, we finally accepted abandoning ourselves to the net of our unstitched lives. The thin mesh of a joy kept secret deep in our sweaters vibrated with their sailor look, the snow crab claws frozen in the containers and the frosty antennas of Sept-Îles shrimp that would leave for Matane then the Metro grocery stores of Montreal with the label "Matane Shrimp." We had a few dollars left for a nightcap in the hotel restaurant, where we surprised the waitress's biting smile behind the plates of cod so nicely decorated by the Madelinot cook—a little carrot for the orange, slivered almonds for the beige, a thin slice of potato like a translucent veil floating over the fillet of fish our grandfather the seagull had fought against before his life as a bird. We were the princes of Laure Boulevard with our sheep's wool hats from Ushant and our trailing purple scarves, a long reflection of distant islands pressing into our eyes the desire to confront the void, boreal dawn astern, feigned calm of travellers who carry trembling deep inside, fears choked back to continue on the way, a seagull on our shoulder.

What happened to the Jonathan Livingston motel? Rivière-au-Tonnerre, thunder river, I love that name so much, red boats alongside the rocks. At the convenience store, this ritual: unroll my horoscope, a little parchment rolled up in a cardboard tube like a lipstick for a doll house—the virgin is crazy, she goes to find love deep in the eyes of an old nomad . . . To each a path. Mine is called Mingan. Route 138, between sea and forest, always the same vertigo, the same sensation of going towards one's self by moving outside of time. Recite by heart: Essipit, Les Escoumins, Forestville, Pessamit, Baie-Comeau, Port-Cartier, Uashat, Sept-Îles, Mishta-shipu, Mani-utenam, Chutes Manitou, Sheldrake, Rivière-au-Tonnerre, Rivière-Saint-Jean, Longue-Pointe-de-Mingan, Ekuanitshit, forget time and the kilometres still to be travelled before the end of the road from which rises a fragrance of home. Realize that this time I'm not asking myself the question "What am I doing here?" For a long time that question has no longer been asked on this route, it is no longer about leaving, it is no longer even about going, or about returning, it's about letting ourselves drift, absorb parts of the self that we have left while wandering in the taiga, when the route vanishes in a crazy gold kiss between the sea foam and the barrens on the round rocks of Sheldrake, say hello to the dead without distinguishing them from the living. Maniten had told Nuenau that I was her first friend among Those who arrived in big wooden canoes. When she departed, without anyone knowing at what age exactly, between ninety and a hundred and ten

years, it was her mother and her grandmother who went to tell
me in the distance. In my dream: two old women of the forests.

Hoping to see the features of the deceased appear in the faces
of the newborns, crossing the bridge of free rivers and harnessed
rivers, meeting special convoys of mobile houses balanced on
the trailers of huge trucks, thinking that a lot of friends will
be doing cleaning or cooking in those trailers on hydroelectric
construction sites while dreaming of going back up those rivers
as far as Ungava Bay. Looking at the sea and accepting that it
is called the sea, even though its colours and its temperature, its
music have nothing to do with those I knew in my childhood,
no longer wondering about the meanings of words, the origins,
the fact that angel cards are next to eagle feathers, stones, books
on opening chakras, drums, teueikanat, and cliffs, as long as we
look at each other around a tea and know how to distinguish
sadness from dismay, as long as we still know how to make
Innu tea with four bags of Salada in a pot of boiling water, lots
of sugar, a bit of warm water. The last time I drank that tea, it
was at a bingo evening, lit candles on the kitchen table to drive
away the smell of cigarettes, the radio full blast on the coun-
ter, and the wireless phone beside Penassin. The jackpot of six
thousand dollars was at stake for numbers 37 or 65. I'd bought a
ten-dollar card and a 50/50 for two dollars. We had gone to the
community radio to get our gridded cards. I play bingo every
ten years. I take it as a mantra. The numbers announced first in
Innu-aimun, then in French, put me in a state close to medita-
tion. "G nishtunnu ashu patetat, G trente-cinq, G nishtunnu
ashu patetat . . . B patetat, B cinq, B patetat . . . I peikunnu

ashu nishuaush, I dix-huit, I peikunnu ashu nishuaush, I dix-huit . . . "I struggled not to fall asleep, that long litany of numbers lulled me so much. Nuenau, who already had three cards to mark, checked that I didn't forget to colour on mine the numbers that were falling. She's the one who noticed that I was missing the number 37 to complete the shape of the letter Y on the third turn. But the telephone rang at the community radio. Someone had won. Goodbye to the jackpot and the new car that for an instant had crossed my mind, a vehicle in good condition to come and see them more often in Ekuanitshit.

"You should've married my father. You'd be a widow now and you'd have a house . . . " Her eyes sparkling, Penassin waits for my reaction. With a wry smile, I reply, "Yeah, that way, you'd be my step-daughter."

The Body of the Forests

October 2010

Nutshimit. A wish fulfilled. I jump out of the Otter and kneel in the bushy carpet of the lichen. For twelve years I've been dreaming of again setting foot in the inland house. Here is where I left the most enraptured part of me, the consciousness of my body. Did I come to get news of the Elders who have gone back to their territory, news of the North, or of myself?

Lake Uauahk stretching out against a backdrop of black spruce and amber larches is where Antoine spent time. His daughter Carole invited us, Nuenau and me, to camp for a week with her and her silent brothers. Manitou's smile, Adrien's slanting eyes, and the raw intensity of the adolescents accompanying them, Tshakapesh, Dave, encourage me to take part in the human chain that carries boxes of provisions, mattresses, and blankets to our already warm tent. The men have lit the stove in anticipation of our arrival. They have woven fir branches on the ground. A fragrance of black honey.

I glimpse navigable dreams in the strength of arms, between

the foot and the head of the lake, a liquid consciousness where survival and love are based on the same impulse. A good hunter loves the animal he kills.

The shadows in the tent reawaken memories of the three months spent a few paddle strokes northwest of here, on Kukamessit, that huge lake as welcoming as a woman's womb. My silhouette from then continues to walk on the spongy paths of lichen in the footprints of solitary caribou. Nutshimit has kept my face intact. I lace on my snowshoes. Tears of light in the ice of the fir trees, the moon . . . Shimun is waiting for me with his axe under the spruce trees, denim game bag on his back. We cut through the night on a single trail open in the fresh snow on the ice of the lake. Broad crack of dawn . . . "Stack the wood at the tent entrance. Help me unfold the mattress. Take only the clothes you need. The rest of them, leave in your bag outside under the plastic." I obey Nuenau's each and every instruction, as before.

When we were on Kukamessit, Nuenau convinced me that Carole's father's nickname was Massenitak. I was calling him "Cutie" without realizing it. Carole gulps. We laugh, but our hearts aren't in it. Sitting down with a cup of tea, we talk about the last days of Shimun and Antoine. They followed one another closely, going off with other "housed" nomads of their generation around the year two thousand. Carole's father had wanted to see his lake again before it was flooded. They were talking about the Churchill Falls II dam project at the time. Kukamessit and Uauahk were in the sights of Hydro-Québec. The mountains were going to become islands. Antoine wanted to see his territory again. Back in the village, he fell ill with cancer. Shimun's had already been detected and he too had returned one last time to his lake with his children, Shamani, Maniu, Shak, Nuenau, and his grandchildren, Lauraine, Christelle, Tania, and Moïse-Pien. Penassin, who had to stay in the community for her work, had organized their journey. Nuenau had helped Shimun, already very weak, to board his canoe. He went off alone on the lake, for a long time, an hour perhaps . . . He came back with a tear in his eye.

Another day, they had gone together to clean up our old campsite. Shimun had not forgotten to take down the little wooden cup that I had hung up, one year before, on a pole in the tent to take the pulse of the seasons in our absence. It had become pale and smooth.

The only way to fill a little that abyss their departure had dug within us was to come back to their lands. I knew it vaguely, but I let myself grow old under feelings of nostalgia. Sometimes I would catch a glimpse of Shimun's smile to rekindle the embers. The memories twist painful old branches inside me. One does not return with impunity to the places of one's happiness.

How could we ignore the fact that a dam was afoot downstream on the Romaine River, which flows a stone's throw from here? The North is the object of all kinds of greed. It's the land that can save us and not the other way around. I share with my friends the presence of their fathers in the tent.

That night, one of us will shed the tears of the mourning that she has never done. The only planet worth visiting is still the one where the force of gravity permits our tears to flow to the earth that drinks them. No struggle, but prayers that we leave under our footsteps and books that are written before the day.

The muffled voices on the CB radio crackle with the rain.

Under the blankets, three sleeping women.

Bring back the names to the forest.

My bear dream: its claws.

The doors open . . .

The light takes shape in the heart of slow stories.

With my whole body, I unfold the mats alongside me on the lake, floating adrift, my heavy breasts giving milk to those improbable stars—the song from the old languishing mountain.

And our night wakes up to the passing of two moose under a sky dappled with soft pink.

> A carton of Grand Pré milk
> *conveniently fresh*
> 2% on the log
> and my boots
>
> first snow
> the lake trout
> doesn't care
>
> under the black sheet of the lake
> the trout dreams me
> fishing pole
>
> fire
> in the woods
> you, alive

> the snow throws
> vanishing lines
> on the canvas of fir trees
> the temptation to disappear
>
> the dogs at bay
> fear of the wolf
> and my desire

Walking along the lake, my thoughts free like a source of wind . . . I join in the conversation of two partridges, each of them on their spruce branch. The desire to share this encounter is stronger than the fear of endangering the lives of those singers by revealing their presence not far from the camp.

"Pineuat tshiapamauat a?"

Adrien puts the .22 rifle in Dave's hand and asks me to show him the way. Even if I say that those birds are sweet-talking each other, that they're in love, it's no use. We are here to hunt and eat that delicious dish.

The young man in camouflage outfit, his moony eyes and me, do not find the two partridges again.

> Our boots in the moss
> shiver of first flakes
> being in this country like in my body.

The tender green of the taiga mosses calms the vertigo of finding oneself in the middle of nowhere, that is, of everything—our position in the world.

When the wind rises, I unravel farther to the north.

The forest is breathing deeply.

"A granite laugh . . . " I open my eyes after reading those words in a dream, the beginning of a tightly-written text that refers to low vegetation and forces received on high plateaux sanded by the winds. I don't know who wrote it, but I get dressed hastily to set out in search of the first trail that in a few metres can take me from the taiga to the tundra.

The crystals of frost clinging to the peat moss make my footsteps crunchy. Between two ravines protecting the last trees before the next latitude, the flesh-coloured, green, and black paintings of the crustose lichens tarnish broad rocky platforms. Those pieces of naked planet skin leave me with the feeling of belonging to an elementary order of which we have forgotten the laws . . .

A little island of lichen in the centre of a stone.

A mineral line separating a rock in the middle as far as the nine-o'clock rays of the sun.

A cloud of tundra plants.

Hairs of moss climbing, in a spiral, around the slender trunk of a black spruce.

The call of a star-studded rock, almost a stela.

The depth of a turquoise spring in the outlines of the forest.

A granite laugh crystallized by the cold.

A dog goes with me everywhere I go.

The moon rises and continues its course.

Nutshimit
vertical density
of spruce trees on a gentle slope

the sea and the forest forces
of the unknown that we tame
according to their rhythm

I write the sea
and I feel the land
the latter is the miracle
of the former.

Time never stops flowing through the branches of the trees
and the black earth, around the lake, drinking too. The sky
wakes us with its spiral forces. There is great thirst to blend with
this euphoria.

One night after
another vanishes
and the day swells

the night envelops us
the dogs keep watch
the land is breathing

the rusty stove pipe
speaks in morse code
to the deaf moon

mouth closed
journeys in the body

utshekatakuat
those who are far

the stars
we dream
that we stem
from the same dream
and everything will be fine.

Wasn't there a time when we moved with bare hands in a canvas of glints to touch the night as if it were day, the door to the next day?

No fear of getting up in the night. Fire, wind, and tea, that rediscovered aroma wakes me at lightning speed down to the tips of my toes.

The canoe speeds to the north of the lake.

Amishku-ishkueu . . . Amishku-ishkueu . . . Amishku-ishkueu . . .

Beaver Woman . . . Shimun was waiting for me. He addresses me affectionately with that nickname that I had forgotten and asks me to remember.

In the forest, we lived, it gave us everything. In the daytime, we would walk. In the evening, we would lie down to find the right path.

The light is a trail. My footsteps silently follow it.

No one will ever again be able to say we are dead.

The Ors

I glimpse the gleaming path
of each sharp the snow makes
being born

MARIE-ANDRÉE GILL

The Old Man

Uashtessiu–pishim[u] 2017

Shimun,
I'm coming back.

Nineteen years have gone by without me returning to Kukamessit to live on the lake and in the forest. The fear of coming face-to-face with what is missing. The old man is gone.

We were beautiful. We were alive. The animals, sometimes, showed themselves to us.

The same route
free

his name
the Earth
covered with night.

A black car comes by to take me to the dawns. In my bag, a thick sleeping bag, a head lamp, a few candles. We laugh with hushed voices.

From Montreal to Ekuanitshit, brush past the St Lawrence, make it into a piece of liquid clothing with which we blend with the forest, rediscover the dull beating of its heart behind each tree, catch the pieces of life that are lying around. Not shouting, from joy or from pain. Thinking about the Bear whose golden claws pierce the night.

"If you see him,
speak to him!"

On the dashboard, a little plastic panda keeps Bernard company. "He's from the same family. If you see him there, in Kukamessit, speak to him. The Bear is a human. He understands when he is spoken to. He must be respected as a member of the family."

Nimushum, my grandfather, is hungry.

Between the mountain
and the river
the clouds sponge
our fevers.

Unroll the ribbon of Route 138. Stop at a Tim's and introduce the bitter taste of an espresso in a cardboard cup to the one driving us to his village. Rediscover Bernard's gravelly voice. Old, old friend.

I've known him all these years, Bernard, summers in Mingan sand and rust, on the radio porches country songs, with the smell of bread under the fire and his blues today washed by long stays in the forest bringing young people back to the source.

"I am a bear."

In the black car, in profile, the resemblance is striking. Bern gave me a thousand-kilometre lift in exchange for coffees. We talk about our mutual friend, Penassin, at whose home we met during my first stay in Ekuanitshit.

Yes, you, my Penassin. You, with your heart of gold, taking in wandering souls. You who was entrusted with the house of the Bear to care for us. You were like a mother to us.

"The Bear especially
understands us."

In a fast-food restaurant in Forestville, we were charged double.
I ask the cashier to make an effort to understand us. We hadn't
ordered that many potatoes.

You remember, Penassin, that love song in Innu-aimun,
repeated over and over again, always the same tune, listened to
again and again as the sun was setting? You loved that Petapan
album. My hair was long and I was trimming the coat of the
little dog Belle with scissors on your porch. The children of
the village brought us poems. Bernard often visited us. Your
father wandered like an old lost bear on the beach. Your father,
Shimun, whose name spoke for itself.

"Kuei nimushum
eka nutshikui nimushum
tshussimish au nin."

"If you run into him, you'll say to him very calmly in our language: Hello, grandfather. Don't worry about me, grandfather, I'm your grandchild. He'll understand you and be on his way." Bernard's voice is soft and low. Hearing those kinship words spoken with so much respect, I almost saw the Bear appear by the side of the road.

Shimun had those mysterious words that he whispered as if to himself when we set out before dawn. The wind was blowing on the riverbank. The trees were bending slightly.

Uashtessiu-pishim[u]
the moon of the luminous land
or else the sun of the shining land.

The larch trees take on a lunar colour. Bernard lets me off in
Sept-Îles. The name of the month of October in Innu-aimun,
Uashtessiu-pishim[u] is also the moon when I plunge into the
forest to see my departed friends again. They are with umushu-
mimau Mashk[u]. They are with the Bear, their grandfather. They
are close to him.

   There are mournings that are done softly, like dreams in the
future.

March sends russet signals and I sink
into a thousand-year sleep until four o'clock
the day bursts in flakes on the window
overheated with skin desires
we are tonight
what we need to be
black stone of the North
and dream of the South
blue grey my
bear shoulder that sleeps
with his hunger.

The sky turns
both eastward and northward
around a bone
that exhausts your gaze by dint
of dreams under
my body

claws
clutching the sun

you growl in me deeply
the murmur of torrents.

I tremble with you
in a shambles of bones
that tremble

your skeleton
is a brother.

Clawed by the Bear
in the sun's fight
to give the night back
to its sand take
shape in your hand
moved by dreams.

I will relearn
our old languages
to be able to say your name
that cannot be spoken
without being exposed
to your strength

Mashk^u
Ors
Arz

Stone bear.

Rising sun
grey mountain

standing on the plain
the gooseberry Bear.

Nuenau meets me at Les Galeries Montagnaises shopping
centre. We buy flour, canned milk, frozen foods, batteries for

the radio, and the powdered chocolate that Shimun always carried in his pouch. We will offer him some there.

Each time we lit a fire on the shore of the frozen lake, the old man would hand me a cup of hot chocolate. We would regain our strength through that ritual.

The wind blows
from the misty sky
five geese
sun sap
northward
the eagle follows them.

Liquid blue sky. The sun surfaces from the Mingan River.
Figures of birds are superimposed beside it, pointing their
beaks towards the morning star.

The day of your burial last spring, Penassin, it was snowing so hard. The storm had covered the village with whiteness.
Just when it was time to close the coffin, I glanced towards the
island, out the window. A flock of geese came to get you.

In the light of dawn
amplified by the mist
of the plains
you smile.

Your photo hanging from the rear-view mirror swings with the twists of the road. Pun is driving. He has these reassuring words: "Laure, look, Penassin is smiling at you, she'll accompany you there, to Kukamessit."

When I arrived at your place, you let me know that the door would always be wide open to me and you would take care of me as your father wished. Death has changed nothing of your promise.

On the water mirror of Lac des Plaines
surrounded by golden taiga,
a Beaver.

We unload the boxes and bags from the back of the pickup, our provisions, our boots, bags of clothes, blankets, radio, maps of the territory, guns, coolers. The pilot of the Beaver has us stand on the scale after weighing the load. Four passengers and a big dog. Our journey weighs seven hundred pounds.

I remember your father Shimun, how happy he was to see the bags, the guns, and the dogs pour into the airplane on the shore of that same lake. His face lit up when arriving on Lac des Plaines, his footsteps strengthened. He again became the man of the situation. He was taking us to his home.

Orphans
of the Universe

we are searching for the Bear
like children
their mother.

An hour and a half flight. Transmission lines scratch the forest. The mountains and the rivers outline the twists and turns into which my love blends, the love from that time when I followed the old man.

On the approach to big Lake Kukamess, which the pilot points out to me in the distance, my heart swells. I spot Nuenau's new camp at the head of the lake. We are two orphans going back to the source.

Grandmother Lake Trout

Kukamess-nipi

The little islands
here and there
those memories.

Touch down. Unload the boxes from the airplane, carry them
to the beach, open the camp, sweep, stow, bring in wood, take
down the canoes from the stilts on which the still fresh antlers of a caribou were hung in expectation of its future spirit
body. Without having long to find my footprint again, I feel
myself wandering in the forest a few metres from my body.
Rain falls on the pale lichens and the leaves of Labrador tea.
I cut branches of fragrant needles. I walk in circles among the
trees. A lake reminds me that we went that way in the past,
your father and I. He had a bout of dizziness.

Nineteen years ago, I was still a little girl and you, Penassin,
an accomplished woman. You accompanied your father for the
first time in his territory and you were radiant. Another man
was revealed behind the paternal figure.

On Lake Élie, Jean killed a moose
we listen to the CB
crackle
heavy rain during the night.

Nuenau lights a few candles on the table. The cloudberry jam melts on slices of homemade bread. The fire is burning in the stove. The old man's photo and yours on a shelf watch over us. I brought back the canvas bag that I had embroidered here. I was twenty-six years old at the time. I'm forty-five. Only the fabric has withstood the years. As soon as the opportunity presents itself, I go back into the matutishan to heal.

The presence of the old man made me happy. I had the feeling I was living through moments that would never be repeated. Without sharing many words of the language of the other, we managed to understand each other through smiles, gestures, improvised dance steps on the ice. He was one of the last of his generation to be born in the woods and to have lived as a nomad. He knew the language of Nutshimit, the laughter of the mountains, the love rituals of the caribou, their moulting to the rhythm of the lunar calendar. In the evening, to the crackling of the radio, he brought us the stories transmitted since millennia by faithfully repeating each word. He imitated the intonations of the person who had told the story before him. He knew things, your father. The land.

"Bury your toothpaste
in the sand, its smell
like marshmallows
attracts bears."

I have lost my reflexes as a daughter of the woods and Nuenau
guides my tiniest gestures. "Your head is always in the clouds."
The moon rises through the clouds from behind a mountain to
the east, the place of the sun. How long did it take him to come
back to the same place? Nineteen years, I believe. Like me. Full
circle. Everything can start again.

In the evening, inside the tent, Shimun told us the story of
Tsheshei, the old man who had escaped death by posing as a
young man.

My grandmothers flakes of wings
cloak me in their flow.

To have a forest speak to you, close your eyes and sing, let the
wind come. The forest, from the roots to the treetops, feels our
presence.

They say, Penassin, that you became a white she-wolf. Your
little sister Nuenau saw you, as recently as a month ago, watching her from the other side of the beach.

Dreamed of Him
black fur
starry body.

The boiling hot coffee, drunk before dawn in a blue metal cup,
the night still heavy, the bodies of the children slumbering
bundled in sleeping bags, and I again see that body of a giant
starry bear in the sky. A cold rain pierces the lake.

I came back to the home of the old man, hoping to meet
him again on the land that he loved the most in his lifetime.
But how to be sure that it's really he who is blowing on my
face? Him or who else? We have the old man in our white hair.
His sidereal fat, diluted within our bodies since the beginning
of the world, cares for us under cave-shaped shelters, carpeted
with fir boughs. Before going into the woods, we entered the
house of the Bear. We carried out a ceremony in the matutishan, of which you were the guardian, in order to receive your
healing and to set out again in Nutshimit. We were six inside,
four women and two men. The rocks brought back by Nuenau
from Kukamessit lit up the night. Extreme heat. You loved
the colour blue and it was with a dark turquoise that the
round tent of the matutishan had been covered, a canvas sewn
with love so that you can find us again each time we enter
the lair of your grandfather. By smearing the bear grease on
my chest, I wanted him to be close to my heart during our
journey. I made sure that he came into my body. We sweated,
sang, prayed. I thanked Nimushum Mashk^u, our grandfather,
and our grandmothers. Luminous cedar on the stones. I was

told that the Bear, in the forest, would appear to me. "He will show himself to you. You mustn't be afraid. The country will take you. Our grandfather wants to take you as his wife."

The rain has soaked
the mattress
of airy
lichen
from the land

liquid footsteps
wet legs.

Rain. Walk in the forest. Gathering ikuta with its powerful, velvety leaves, to make Labrador tea. Lichens, mosses, orangish mushrooms, blueberries, spruce, larch, fragrance of the spirits. The root of the Bear penetrates the stone and my body through my nostrils. Caribou trails flare out across the North from the head of Kukamess-nipi. Scattered shreds of tobacco. Nuenau's young golden retriever catches up with me. Its name is Tushis. The little dog of the old man, however, has been dead for seventeen years. Presence of the dog in the dog.

From here, no one has ever left.

"The moon in the middle of the lake
three stars
it's going to be nice tomorrow"
Nuenau wakes me up at three o'clock in the morning.

So calm, so big. A lake or the Universe. Tame your fear. The children are asleep. I go with Nuenau to the porch. The sky is clear. For a long time we've been promising each other we'd return together to Kukamessit . . .

We often speak your first names as talismans. Penassin, Shimun taught you to steer the canoe on this starry lake. The childhood you did not know has finally been given back to you. You had had a tea on a beach, eaten dried caribou meat on slices of bannock. A white-headed eagle had flown over you. Shimun had told you about a bear den a little to the north, not far from the place where we made camp today. Last winter, it left claw marks on the trees on the north side of the camp.

Forest of mosses
on the white waking.

The night fades step by step cracking lichens pale with frost. A red sun rumbles under the land. The dog, with me, prowls. The dog doesn't care at all about my quest, about my sorrows. He wants to play at running, at tracking down partridges, sniffing out hares or bears, whatever. Jump higher than the caribou, yes, he really likes that. I ponder, between the two lakes, the weight of the moon and of the sun, the absence of the old man, the hope of the old bear.

Knife cut in the white antler of the caribou—a single object received from her grandfather wards off fear.

Spirit of the forest
a love
body.

Blueberries roll in the hollow of my hand, sometimes the Bear
is happy to know that a female gathers blueberries for him in
the purple life of one morning. With each step, the sound of
lichens bursts stars in my brain numb with cold, the breathing of the old man. The dog sniffs out trails and I have no rifle.
The bear voice comes back to our consciousness, root. Find the
den. Constellation of tobacco on the water. That the Old Man
sniffs. Return in zigzags between the lakes. And all those trees
that look alike. The dog. The partridge. The river. The sun is no
longer on my left but on my right. I've changed direction and
recognize nothing. Moss lichen spruce wood. I chew Labrador
tea leaves. Wander in the forest full of whispers. Dance of balance between the worlds. I go round in circles. I've been walking for at least three hours. What are you asking me? From
shoulders to claws, a growl. I come back a woman, where I shed
my childhood like an old skin. It puts the light back in the path
of my head. Lay down your eyelids. Choose the wind. Go down
into the cave of your body. Heal.

    Nimushum, tanite etain? I am your grandchild.

The Bear
eats
my hunger.

Lost amongst the lakes. In the distance, Kukamessiuutshu. My legs wet from following the dog in the river, sure that he knew the way back—he only wanted to have some more fun—I walked to the south until I could no longer go on at the end of that spit of land. If I got lost, I should take the peaks of the Kukamess mountains as landmarks and they would show me the south, Shimun had repeated to me.

The little islands with tall poles of spruce trees floating in the mist reminded me of the sea when we arrived on the big lake by canoe. They imprinted themselves on me so much that one day they gave my son his second name, Minishtikuss, Little Island. I must have gone past the camp without seeing it. I've walked too far south.

Hot day
never has a fire
smelled so good to me

my clothes are drying on the line
lustre of the land.

Breakfast eggs, cheeses, toast, coffee. We stack the wood.
Pragmatic as always, Nuenau remarks to me in her loudest
voice, half-jokingly as if to ward off fate, "If we'd had to go
searching for you by helicopter, who would have paid for it?
When an Innu gets lost, it's the council that pays, but you?" I
don't have the strength to try to find out. Arm to the sky, "I'd
be dead in the woods, that's all there is to it." And confess to
her how crazy it was to go off without telling anyone, without
provisions or a walkie-talkie. A small island saved me. I promise
her to never again plunge into the forest alone. We will walk
together. Let myself be carried. I'll trust in the present moment.
Will relearn the Innu art of living.

　　The Bear gave me the greatest lesson of humility.

Fragmented with stars
vibrant with sky.

Night of hot stars. Threads to embroider deep blue, turquoise, red, purple. Tracks of animal feet. Bear. Forward, forward on the embroidery, the long cloth that links us to the world above. Communication channel between two worlds bound by shapes and colours, aromas. Sweetgrass. My spine sways with the wind. The Bear forms a stellar hurricane.

The sky with a heartbeat roll.

Gilding of wind
offered on the lake

the waves that create our voices
from south to north.

Nuenau is singing on the beach. Her tremolos penetrate the air.
I feel she's calling to you without trying to hold on to you. A
powerful wave runs across the lake.

Two eagles.

By boat
on the big lake
the little islands
that capsize me.

Rain, wind on Pikuanipanan and all the places where, with Shimun, we had paddled. A light sun emerges from the clouds. Jean, my grandfather become Chinese through his painting teachers, had laid down on a canvas the pearly water of Kukamess-nipi on the basis of a few words that I had written to him. If he had not gone to the world of stars, today would be his birthday. The spruce trees on the little islands remind me of Jean's brush stroke. Pikuanipanan, the Place where one breaks through the ice in winter to spread the net, remembers Shimun's paddle stroke. My grandfathers and my child, my compasses in the circle of time.

The Bear loves our children as his grandchildren.

Airy snow
light sun
cold wind
waves in boat
spurt in the face

an eagle beats us
to our old camp.

Nuenau uprights Shimun's sled faded by the years against the pole of an old tent. On our knees, where we once slept and dreamed, I tremble with my whole body from the memory of the land. Two young fir trees have grown in the place where our heads rested at night. Ebb from my youth, the tenderness of the old man. I tie a piece of red wool to the trunk of the little fir trees so they know I came back. The boat crosses unexpected clouds of snow in the shining autumn. It plunges into a stream covered with larch needles. Kneeling in the bow, I measure the depth using a paddle. Nuenau has the map of the territory imprinted in her flesh; from lake to lake, she guides us under the snow-fragranced sun. If I had not had the feeling of having recovered an ancient dazzled force, I could have believed we dreamed those moments.

We have to become what we are. Forget everything. Love, Love, Love. The wind of Nutshimit has some of those words flown away from the memory of the land.

Red
clouds
in the lake

soon the sun
will emerge from the mountain
as if from a skin.

Nutshimit, your big heart scents my lungs. Each new day has its colour, its promise of encounters written in the nuances of the wind. Yesterday we returned to our old campsite and we crossed a cloud of snow. Last night, I dreamed of the Bear our grandfather. He was old and gentle. He was beside a porcupine. That very same porcupine, the first animal I killed under Shimun's proud and amused gaze.

You taught me the dreams.

The black mountain
purple reflection on the lake

a fish breaks through
the golden layer of light

on the shore the lichen
cracks with frost.

Go fetch water from the spring. Gather the ikuta in the shape of little canoes, those grandmother leaves that heal us, take care of the brilliance of our eyes, wash our words.

During a healing ceremony to which you had invited me, your father appeared. He spoke to the guide, who did not dare to repeat his surprising words. Shimun looked him in the eyes and, with a strong gesture of the finger, ordered him to do it: "Tell her! The young woman sitting in the corner, the one who comes from the other side of the sea, tell her that she hasn't changed in all this time and that I'd be happy to marry her." Your father hasn't changed either. He has not lost a bit of his sense of humour.

Nikushpian
I go back to the source
I breathe every second.

Dreamed of a handsome young man. Shall we go see a caribou? Checked snares. Fetched water by canoe in the lake. Contemplation near Pakatak, the lake without tributaries. Tidying. Pancakes with partridgeberry jam.

Tonight, my life is a forest.

The night gathers me
scattered pieces to repair
like a forest that we wrap
in a bear pelt.

"The hot coals and the embers were making funny glimmers inside the tent. It was very beautiful. It was our light." Nuenau reads me a passage from the only book she brought with her to the woods, the *Récits de Mathieu Mestokosho* (*Caribou Hunter: A Song of a Vanished Innu Life*), the stories of her great-uncle. "That evening, the weather was gloomier than ever. The sky had completely clouded over. My grandfather said that when a bear died the weather always turned bad. It was night and we were sleeping in the tent. In the middle of the night someone shouted that it was snowing really hard. We had been buried by the snow, which was as high as the roof of the tent. We had to dig ourselves out. We said to each other that only the bear could have done something like this." Her reading brought back memories. Before the alternation of the seasons, recounted Shimun, winter went on and on and threatened to extinguish life on the land. The Bear was the sole guardian of the warmth, which he kept in a skin hanging from a tree on an island. A squirrel managed to make a hole in the upper wall of the world. The Bear covered up the breach, which pierced the sky, with a heavy hide.

If we have hair on our heads it's maybe to keep us from escaping through space.

Wait for the old
man who is sleeping
to come to you.

I write this phrase on the inside of my left wrist before going
to sleep and a storm rages in my head. Full sky. Land strength.
Battle between a bear and a dog. Fight to the death. Which
could have happened if I had run into it the day when I got lost.
It's nothing but the wind . . . No, it's Nutshimit speaking to us
in spirit. The night is a fireplace of dreams. Time, when it flares
out from the fire of the stove, shimmers around your sleeping
body.

I fell into a void of time, at the end of the loop that closes
better to be released. Nineteen years to be reborn. I am trans-
planted with a second heart—it will beat to the rhythm of the
forest. Tshimeshkanam, tshimeshkanam, tshimeshkanam . . . A
night of love in the voices. I wake up to the light sound of a
drum, feeling as if I've returned to the luminous forest to speak
to my grandfather, my heart washed.

Come out of dawn
arms full
of mountains

underground, the night breathes.

Natamit, the West. Natuaten, I search. Natuatum, she searches.
Nanitem, always. Nimushuminan, our grandfather. The rifle
with the wear of Shimun's hands on Nuenau's shoulder, we go
around the back of the lake on the paths dug by the caribou—
Nuenau sings for Papakassik[u]—he sinks his hooves into the airy
moss, that tender green lichen he enjoys eating. This forest is a
nest into which you sink your life to heal your heart. I notice a
long, wide rock, northwest, perhaps a lair.

   All the stories have bodies. You have that wind that fills. The
path of the sky, a mind-body.

In the skin cooked
in the fire of the land
feed the child.

A rock facing the setting sun. A red fabric filled with tobacco for Nimushum. Our grandfather is preparing for winter. His walk is heavy and calm. He will sleep facing west and the heat of the sun will be swallowed up in his fur. The vapour of his breathing, through the tunnel that he's taken care to dig, will melt a circle of snow on the upper wall of his lair. He will turn over only twice during his hibernation. The second time will signal the arrival of spring.

Don't forget that the old man weeps when you forget to talk to him. The solitude of a grandfather. He will show himself to you when you really need him. Introduce yourself to him in the night. Fill his cavern with offerings. Feel the sky in your palms when you give them to him. The spirit of the forest, constellation of blue-green lights, welcomes the phrases of your heart, moves as fast as the name is thrown to the mosses, the stars. I still live among you.

Song of the loon
where the beaver swims
a larch.

Tshimishakamein. You come to the end of your journey by
canoe.

   Among the starburst needles of the larch, you set forth,
Penassin, oh . . .

Old Woman,
your breath
fills the forest

where the sky cleaves
the land, we're
your descendants.

References

The sections "The Sky," "The Sea," "The Land," and "The Fire" have sources in the book *La Route des vents* [The Route of the Winds] (Rennes, La Part commune, 2002, revised, corrected and supplemented in 2015).

The section "The Ors" was first published under the title "Le vieil homme" ("The Old Man") in the collective work *Oùrs* (Marie-Andrée Gill, Mahigan Lepage, Sébastien Ménard, and Laure Morali, Montréal: Possibles Éditions, 2019).

A passage from the chapter "Mishta-meshkanu, la grande route, la 138" ["Mishta-meshkanu, the Highway, the 138"] appears in the book *Comment va le monde avec toi* (Montpellier: Publie.net, coll. "La machine ronde," 2013).

The poem "À l'extrême nord du monde" ["At the northern extreme of the world"] (p 65) is taken from *L'Étoile polaire* by Yvon Le Men (Vénissieux: Paroles d'aube, 1998).

The quotations by Mathieu Mestokosho (p 146) come from the book *Récits de Mathieu Mestokosho, chasseur innu* by Serge Bouchard (Montréal: Boréal, 2004; coll. "Boréal compact," 2017). English translation: *Caribou Hunter: A Song of a Vanished Innu Life*, translated by Joan Irving (Greystone Books, 2006).

Acknowledgements

I wish to thank Shimun Pashin, Nuenau Mestokosho, Penassin Pashin, and their extended family, from the Innu community of Ekuanitshit and Nutshimit, for the paths and the laughter shared in a spirit of friendship; Rita Mestokosho and Jean-Charles Piétacho for their luminous preface; Louis Hamelin for his inspiring invitation to be part of the collection "L'oeil américain"; Mahigan Lepage, director of the collection "La machine ronde" chez Publie.net, Guillaume Martel LaSalle, Catherine Langlais of Possibles Éditions, and Mireille Lacour of Éditions La Part commune for being open to allowing the texts published by them to continue on their path.

Originally from Brittany, France, Laure Morali is the author of several short story collections, novels, and poetry collections. She lives in Montreal. Her anthology *Aimititau! Parlons-nous!* (2017) helped strengthen the ties between Quebec's Indigenous and non-Indigenous writers.